Moving With Purpose

Related HighScope Press Preschool Resources

Making Connections: Movement, Music & Literacy

Cultures and Styling in Folk Dance

Rhythmically Moving 1–9 (CDs)

Beginning Folk Dances With Phyllis Weikart (6 DVD set)

85 Engaging Movement Activities
(Learning on the Move, K–6 Series), with attached CD

Round the Circle: Key Experiences in Movement for Children, Second Edition

Movement Plus Music: Activities for Children Ages 3 to 7, Third Edition, with attached CD

Movement Plus Rhymes, Songs, & Singing Games, with attached CD

Movement in Steady Beat, Second Edition
(Learning on the Move, Age 3–7 Series), with attached CD

Available from

HighScope Press
600 North River Street, Ypsilanti, Michigan, 48198-2898
ORDERS: phone 800.400.PRESS; fax 800.442.4FAX
e-mail: press@highscope.org
Web site: www.highscope.org

LEARNING ON THE MOVE

Grades K–5

Moving With Purpose

54 Activities for Learning, Fitness, and Fun

Karen S. Sawyers
With Ellen Colley and
Linda Icaza

HIGHSCOPE
PRESS®

Ypsilanti, Michigan

Published by
HighScope® Press
A division of the
HighScope Educational Research Foundation
600 North River Street
Ypsilanti, Michigan 48198-2898
734.485.2000, FAX 734.485.0704
Orders: 800.40.PRESS; Fax: 800.442.4FAX; www.highscope.org
E-mail: *press@highscope.org*

Editor: Jennifer Burd

Cover design, text design, production: Judy Seling, Seling Design

Photography: Bob Foran, p. 30 (top) and p. 39 (top); all other photos, Karen S. Sawyers.

Library of Congress Cataloging-in-Publication Data
Sawyers, Karen S., 1962-
Moving with purpose : 54 activities for learning, fitness, and fun / Karen S. Sawyers with Ellen Colley and Linda Icaza.
p. cm.
Includes bibliographical references.
ISBN 978-1-57379-473-2 (soft cover : alk. paper) 1. Movement education--Study and teaching (Elementary) 2. Physical education for children--Study and teaching (Elementary) 3. Education, Elementary--Activity programs. I. Colley, Ellen. II. Icaza, Linda. III. Weikart, Phyllis S., 1931- IV. Title.
GV452.S293 2010
372.86--dc22

2009046554

Printed in the United States of America
10 9 8 7 6 5 4 3 2 1

This book is dedicated to my parents,
Leonard and Jean Sawyers. Thank you for
all the memories. I always felt so much
love from both of you!

Contents

Acknowledgments

Note: *Chapters 1–3 were written by Karen S. Sawyers. All the activities were written by Ellen Colley, Linda Icaza, and Karen Sawyers. Phyllis S. Weikart is the author of the dances included in Chapters 4 and 5.*

The authors express their deepest appreciation to Phyllis S. Weikart for her willingness to share her knowledge and experience. Further, the authors express gratitude for her program *Education Through Movement (ETM),* which has provided them with a lifelong journey that has helped to change their lives, and the lives of the children they have worked with, forever.

From Karen S. Sawyers:

I would like to express my sincere thanks to Linda Icaza and Ellen Colley for sharing my vision to write this book and for the years of support! I am grateful to them for opening up their classrooms and sharing their experiences to make this project a reality.

I would like to acknowledge the faculty, students, and parents of Edgewater Elementary in Pensacola, Florida, and Freeman's Mill Elementary in Lawrenceville, Georgia, for their participation in this project. A special thank you to Marian Hicks, Principal of Freeman's Mill Elementary, and Steven Schubert, Principal of Edgewater Elementary, for allowing me to spend time in their schools and work with their students and teachers. Thanks to both of these principals for their support of Linda Icaza (Freeman's Mill Elementary) and Ellen Colley (Edgewater Elementary) during this project.

I would like to thank all the Movement and Music field consultants and trainers for their support and insights during the development of the *Education Through Movement* program. The sharing of ideas and experiences over the years continues to help us shape this program.

I would also like to thank the HighScope staff for their encouragement during the development of this product. Thank you for always finding time to allow me to discuss ideas out loud.

Thanks to all of my friends for their support throughout the years, believing in me when I picked up and moved to Michigan to become involved with *Education Through Movement* and HighScope.

A special thank you to Lisa Jernigan Whitworth for using Phyllis Weikart's materials and convincing me to attend ETM training so many years ago. When I was searching for something to improve my teaching, Lisa helped me find the way to a program that changed the way I work with students. It also changed my career!

Deepest appreciation to Nancy Brickman, HighScope Director of Publications, and to Editor Jennifer Burd and Publications Assistant Katie Bruckner for their help on this project.

Finally, I would like to acknowledge my mother for her support of my decision to move from Tennessee to work at HighScope in Ypsilanti, Michigan. The miles were never able to break the bond we had as mother and daughter; I think of her every day and know that her strength and love will always keep me going.

From Linda Icaza:

I would like to express my deepest appreciation for Connie Wright, whose mentorship was crucial to my contribution to this project. Many of the teaching ideas I contributed came from our work together as teachers. She modeled master teaching for me, and I learned so much from her.

I would also like to thank Karen Sawyers and Ellen Colley, my collaborators on this book, for their gift of friendship, their patience, and their desire to share their vast knowledge.

Thanks also to Dee Glenn, my teaching partner whom I depend on every day to keep me in line. She is always there for me.

Finally, my gratitude goes to Beth Bryant, my closest confidant and the best listener I have ever known.

From Ellen Colley:

I would like to thank M.J. Ziemba for her support and encouragement throughout my *Education Through Movement* training adventure.

I would also like to thank Janet Hutson-Brandhagen and Sue Gerdes for helping me get to Michigan for my first summer training. I would like to thank Karen Sawyers, Liz Harasksin, and Janet for guiding me through the dancing and singing, looking past my inadequacies, and seeing my potential. A big thank you to Linda Icaza and Karen Sawyers for the opportunity to work on this project. This experience has allowed me to gain valuable knowledge and experiences working with the ETM process. Most importantly, thank you for your friendship.

My appreciation to the Weikart Family Foundation for the opportunity to become a field consultant.

Finally, I would like to thank my family and friends for their love and encouragement through the years, even when they didn't "get" what I was doing — they have always been supportive because they know I believe the ETM active learning process gives children the best opportunity for learning.

1
Introduction

When I was in middle school, I decided I wanted to be a teacher. My desire was to work with students and experience the excitement on their faces when they were successful...when they "got it"! So, I finished high school and four years of college, and I became a physical education teacher. However, only about a week into my first teaching assignment, at the age of 21, I realized that I knew *what* to teach but that I didn't know *how* to teach. Some say that mastering the art of teaching is mostly a matter of getting experience under your belt. Indeed — as with so many other professions — effective "on-the-job training" is imperative for success in teaching. This book will help you build on your classroom teaching experience by offering strategies used in HighScope's *Education Through Movement (ETM)* program. This program was developed by Phyllis S. Weikart, one of the country's leading authorities on movement and recreational folk dance.

I learned about the ETM program as I searched for information and strategies that would support and improve my work with elementary school students, especially students in grades K–2. I found myself struggling to find an effective way to teach kindergarten children. I had been working with them as if they were just small fifth graders and, of course, I quickly learned that this approach was not effective. I had no idea of what was developmentally appropriate for that age. I would show students what to do as I talked about it and then expect them to be able to do it the first time they tried, never realizing that they were not yet capable of the task I was demonstrating because it was not developmentally appropriate. I had been teaching seven years when

This teacher and student are working together during a balance activity.

I attended my first ETM training course. The information shared during this training really made sense to me, and it was easy to incorporate in my classroom. During the next 10 years, I used the ETM strategies and content to support and enhance my physical education curriculum. I no longer wondered what to "teach" students, because I had learned how to become a partner in their learning. In this book, you will learn how letting students explore movement, working with students as a partner, and using the *Education Through Movement* teaching model can enhance learning.

What This Book Has to Offer

This book is intended as a K–5 resource for the classroom teacher, to incorporate movement into his or her teaching, and for the physical educator, to use more movement exploration before going into skill development. These strategies and activities will help teachers prepare children for a lifetime of physical activity. Based on ETM teaching methods, the strategies and activities in the book are designed to supplement your physical education curriculum and help you get children moving purposefully through all parts of the daily schedule, from planned movement and music activities to transitions that occur between one part of the day and the next. The activities will give you ideas for working with children at their current developmental level. Note, however, that the activities in Chapters 4 and 5 are presented in alphabetical order, *not* according to developmental sequence. See Appendix C for a chart that identifies related activities.

As you begin working as a partner with students, you will help students explore movement in their own way, to their own timing. Each activity is based on an "essential question." For example, for the first activity in Chapter 4, "Balance," the essential question is "What does it mean to balance?" You can use your students' answers to the essential question to facilitate the activity. That is, their answer will help you understand the students' level of development with regard to a particular movement concept and help you know when to clarify something the students don't understand. My hope is that you will be able to begin using these strategies and activities immediately to create a successful learning environment. Albert Einstein said, "I never teach my pupils; I only attempt to provide the conditions in which they can learn" (The Quotations Page, 2009). I hope this book helps you provide the conditions in your classroom needed for students to feel safe to explore, experience, and be successful in learning!

How This Book Is Organized

This book's easy-to-follow guidelines and activities will help you improve and increase your students' movement experiences as you plan and carry out activities in the classroom each day. It is recommended that you read Chapters 1–3 before using the activities in your classroom. Here is what you'll find in each chapter of this book:

Chapter 1: Introduction. In the remainder of this introduction, we will take a look at why movement experiences are so important for students, with benefits from improved health to better academic performance.

Chapter 2: Getting Students Involved. This chapter explains how you can effectively teach students through exploration and by supporting the students at their level of development. This chapter offers strategies that will help you as you demonstrate skills to students. Techniques explained are based on the ETM model, with examples provided.

Chapter 3: Ways We Move Our Bodies. In this chapter, we discuss the different ways we move our bodies and the movement learning experiences that are key to students' physical, social, and cognitive development. Different types of movement (e.g., locomotor and nonlocomotor) are described in detail, along with strategies for supporting students who are learning and

Providing students with opportunities to share their ideas adds to their engagement and involvement in the activity.

experimenting with different movements. Associated terminology is also given. At the end of the chapter you will find an explanation of the activities in Chapters 4 and 5, with suggestions for helping students get the most out of the activities.

Chapter 4: Activities for Grades K–2. This chapter gives you activities covering a variety of movement content for students in kindergarten through grade 2. From "Making Body Shapes" to "Jumping and Landing," to "Weight Transfer Sequences," to "Space Exploration," you can keep your elementary students moving with purpose throughout the daily schedule! See pages 37–39 for more on how the activities are structured.

Chapter 5: Activities for Grades 3–5. In this chapter you'll find movement activities for older elementary students, including dances. Activities such as "Dribbling to a Steady Beat," "Fitness Ball," and "Balance That Math," and dances such as "Irish Stew" and "The Hustle" will give you many ways to keep students in grades 3–5 happily learning new movement skills!

Other resources in this book. At the end of the book, you'll find a glossary of movement terms used in the activities, a subject index, and a list of the musical selections on the accompanying CD. These selections are suggested for use in some of the activities. Additionally, Appendix A provides a reproducible page of blank "beat boxes" for students to use in choreography to create movement sequences to music for some of the activities in Chapter 5; Appendix B offers a complete "language-to-dance vocabulary" guide for using the dance activities in Chapter 5; Appendix C gives you a chart showing related activities for Chapters 4 and 5; and Appendix D includes a pattern for making a "pumpkin ball" — a soft cloth ball that can be used in the punting activity (Activity 23) in Chapter 5.

Why Is it Important to Get Students Up and Moving?

What the Research Says

Research by Eric Jensen, who studies the brain, shows that physical activity such as moving, stretching, and walking can actually enhance the learning process (Jensen, 2000). Jensen also points out that long periods of seated learning can have ill effects on the hippocampus, a structure in the brain responsible for processing and routing information to other areas of the brain for long-term memory. So it is important for classroom teachers to get students out of their chairs and moving their bodies throughout the day.

Jensen (2000) has also identified several reasons why we should have students move more to learn more:

As students move in different ways, they gain experiences that are key to their physical, social, and cognitive development.

- Movement increases heart rate and circulation and allows more oxygen to go to key brain areas. Stretching increases the cerebrospinal fluid flow to crucial areas of the body.
- Movement gives young learners a new spatial reference for the learning environment. "The brain forms maps, not only on the basis of the scenery, but also from the body's relationship to the scenery. More locations provide more unique learning addresses" (p. 34).
- "Our brains are designed to learn short bursts of information followed by time to process the information... Evidence suggests that time spent not learning new content is very important" (Pelligrini, Huberty, & Jones, 1995, as cited in Jensen, 2000, p. 34). Movement activities can give students and teachers a break.
- As we grow up, our brains change and grow. Students' brains undergo neural pruning (the elimination of existing synapses), neurogenesis (the growth of new brain cells, and myelination (the strengthening of existing neural pathways). Sometimes neural tissue doubles in size in a given area of the adolescent brain, whereas other areas shrink. "This massive change results in an even greater need for content breaks for cognitive remapping" (p. 34). The nervous system does not mature until somewhere between 15 and 20 years of age.
- "Certain kinds of movements can stimulate the release of the body's natural motivators. Two of the best are noradrenaline (the hormone of risk or urgency) and dopamine (the neurotransmitter producing good feelings)" (p. 34). Dopamine can be triggered through gross motor repetitive movements. These energizers wake up students, increase their energy levels, and improve their brain's information storage and retrieval in addition to making them feel good.

Giving Students Opportunities to Explore

Many times we as teachers tend to try to control our class or a particular situation in our classroom. We do not want things to get "out of hand." Because of our fears of losing control of the class, or due to our lack of experience, we may not allow children the opportunity to explore movement concepts or basic abilities in their own timing or in their own way. I have found

Keeping activities simple and allowing students to explore helps the students stay engaged and experience success.

over the years that **being consistent** and **keeping it simple** help to improve classroom management and create an environment for children to feel safe and experience success. Following these guidelines will enable you to plan movement activities that engage students immediately and ensure their success. According to the *American Heritage Dictionary, Second College Edition,* the word *simplify* means "to make simple or simpler; render less complex or intricate" (p. 1142). This is exactly what we try to do as we prepare activities for students. In our lesson plans we think about how we can break down concepts and skills. We begin with simpler strategies and then build to the concept or skill we are trying to present. Students need opportunities to explore and play with movement concepts — space awareness, body awareness, and their relationship to their body and to objects — before they can begin to master motor skills.

As this child participates in a fitness routine, she develops healthy habits that will serve her a lifetime.

Movement for Health

It doesn't matter what subject you teach — it is important to provide breaks for your students and get them out of their seats. According to media reports, childhood obesity has become a nationwide epidemic and a major health threat — dramatically increasing the incidence of cardiac problems, diabetes, and even some forms of cancer. According to the U.S. Surgeon General, nearly 15% of all children and adolescents are dangerously overweight (U.S. Department of Health and Human Services, 2009). Nutritionists talk about "energy in" and "energy out," which describes the balance between calories consumed and calories burned. If a person's physical activity level is not great enough to burn the amount of calories they take in, their weight increases. If this imbalance continues, obesity may result.

Physical education alone cannot solve the problem of obesity, but it is a great place to start. The U.S. Department of Health and Human Services recommends, "Children and adolescents should do 60 minutes (1 hour) or more of physical activity daily" (DHHS, 2008). The National Association for Sport and Physical Education (NASPE) further recommends, "Children should participate in several bouts of physical activity lasting 15 minutes or more each day" (NASPE, 2003). Many school districts are cutting funding for physical education programs; therefore, the classroom teacher can become an important motivator for students to be physically active. Students need time to move and explore the world around them. Encouraging students to be physically active as they explore and follow their interests is very important for developing life-changing healthy behaviors. As educators, we need to find ways to help increase the amount of physical activity that students experience each day.

You already have standards that you use as guidelines in your teaching. In the sidebar, right, you'll find the National Standards for Physical Education developed by NASPE. In an effort to help you meet these standards, each activity in this book lists the NASPE standards that are met by the activity.

Now you know more about why it is so important to get students moving throughout the day. In the next two chapters, we will discuss strategies for getting your students involved and keeping them involved. We will discuss motor development and explore how students develop from using simple to more complex movements. And we will talk about how to extend the students' movement experiences by fostering their creativity and skill in basic timing.

These students are participating in an activity that meets several of the National Standards.

National Standards for Physical Education

Physical activity is critical to the development and maintenance of good health. The goal of physical education is to help individuals develop the knowledge, skills, and confidence to enjoy a lifetime of physical activity.

A physically educated person

Standard 1: Demonstrates competency in motor skills and movement patterns needed to perform a variety of physical activities.

Standard 2: Demonstrates understanding of movement concepts, principles, strategies, and tactics as they apply to the learning and performance of physical activities.

Standard 3: Participates regularly in physical activity.

Standard 4: Achieves and maintains a health-enhancing level of physical fitness.

Standard 5: Exhibits responsible personal and social behavior that respects self and others in physical activity settings.

Standard 6: Values physical activity for health, enjoyment, challenge, self-expression, and/or social interaction.

Source: National Association for Sport and Physical Education (NASPE; 2004, p. 11).

2
Getting Students Involved

The Teaching Model

I hear...I forget.

I see...I remember.

I do...I understand.

— Chinese Proverb

It is important to get students involved and keep them involved throughout the lesson and/or activity. In this chapter, we look at a few important strategies for doing this. In particular, we find the three main components of the *Education Through Movement* teaching model — **separate, simplify,** and **facilitate** — to be very helpful in delivering information to students. Each component is important to getting the attention of students and keeping them involved throughout an activity. The first two components — **separate** and **simplify** — are strategies you can use in presenting concepts and skills. You can use the strategies when planning and initiating activities. The third component, **facilitate**, has to do with our interactions with students. We'll start by taking a look at each of these components.

The *Education Through Movement (ETM)* Teaching Model

To work as a partner with students, use the following strategies:

Separate: Demonstrate, or give verbal directions, or use hands-on guidance.

Simplify: Begin with what is easy or manageable to learn.

Facilitate: Help students think about, describe, and perform their movements.

Separate

The **separate** component involves initiating experiences or presenting information by using only one of the following modes of presentation at a time: **visual** (demonstration), **aural** (verbal directions), or **kinetic** (hands-on guidance). By choosing to separate (i.e., using only one of these three modes of presentation at a time), you enable students to focus on a single message. Combining two or more modes of presentation, such as telling while showing, usually gives students too much sensory input, and some students may miss the information entirely because of the confusion of using two sensory modes at once. For example, telling students how to swing a bat while showing them how to do it can be confusing. Students will be more successful if you *separate* the presentation by either providing visual directions (demonstrating a movement without speaking), or verbal directions (telling students what to do with words only, no movement). It is important, however, to maintain an appropriate balance between visual and verbal directions, and not use just one mode all the time.

Examples of the *Separate* Component

Examples of visual separating (demonstration)

- The teacher gets the students' attention with a statement such as "Watch and copy" before showing students the movements. The teacher puts his or her hands on a long-handled object, such as a golf club, to show hand position while not talking. The students copy.
- The teacher in the classroom writes information on the whiteboard and does not speak while writing, allowing students to read the information without the distraction of the teacher's voice.

As this teacher models the components of the golf swing, she is using the teaching strategy of "visual separate," or separating the visual component of the instruction from the verbal and hands-on components.

Examples of verbal separating

- The teacher gets students' attention with a statement such as "Listen and do" before giving verbal directions. The teacher says, "Wrap both hands on the golf club." The students act upon this direction without the teacher showing the movement. Verbal separating gives the teacher feedback on how students are processing verbal directions.
- The classroom teacher tells the students what the next activity will be before passing out the handouts.

Examples of hands-on guidance

- The teacher asks a student's permission to take the student's hands and put them on the golf club in the correct position.
- The teacher helps a student learn to tie his shoe by taking his hands and helping him to make the loop with the shoestring.

This teacher uses hands-on guidance to help the student balance on his hands and feet.

Simplify

This component involves beginning with what is easy for students or manageable for them to process, allowing students to become immediately engaged and experience success. To simplify, first consider the students' current capabilities and skills. Next, determine the concepts needed for the particular task or skill you want to help the students develop, using your knowledge of prerequisite skills. Then, taking this information into account, determine which concepts or skills are appropriate to the developmental level of the students, and begin there. It is very important that you as the teacher always model or initiate the simplest movement appropriate for the students' developmental level as you work with concepts to develop skills. For example, if you are working with students on locomotor movements, you would demonstrate marching, which is the simplest locomotor movement. Once the students have an understanding of the task, turn the activity over to the students to share ideas, movements, and thoughts.

After the teacher says "watch and copy," students join in following her movement sequence.

Facilitate

This component of the teaching model deals with the ways you involve students through action, thought, and language to support them in constructing their own knowledge. Many times as educators we ask students to listen, copy, perform, participate, and take tests. We are in such a hurry to make sure we include everything we want students to learn that we don't allow students time to share, think, review, reflect, or wonder. Asking open-ended questions (those that don't have a right or wrong answer) helps students develop their thoughts and leads students to a higher level of understanding. This kind of questioning is a great tool for promoting creative thought, problem-solving skills, and cognitive growth in students because it prompts them to spend more time contemplating their responses instead of just giving a disconnected yes or no answer. Open-ended questions allow many more students to talk, because there are many appropriate responses. This in turn allows teachers to learn more about the students. An example of an open-ended question is "How is striking a ball with a racket similar to or different from throwing a ball?"

We as teachers further become partners in learning with students when we encourage students to talk about what they are going to do (plan), to describe what they are doing (do), and to reflect on what they did (review). Results from HighScope's Training for Quality study show that "opportunities for planning and recall were the two dimensions of program quality for children" (Epstein, 1993).

As teachers we want to facilitate throughout the lesson. For example, in the beginning of a lesson we might ask the students a question to determine their level of knowledge or understanding of a certain topic. When students are working on a particular concept and their bodies are moving, we might ask students, "What does your body have to do to move in that way"? At the end of a lesson we may ask a facilitating question to encourage students to apply their knowledge to a different situation. For example, if students have been studying pathways, we might ask, "What are some pathways you have to move in when you get out of bed?"

The teacher asks an essential question at the beginning of the activity to gain students' interest and find out what they know about the subject.

When we **separate, simplify,** and **facilitate**, we provide an interactive environment, that is, one in which the teachers and students work as partners and support one another in the learning process. When teachers work alongside students, the students feel more comfortable and safe. This is an atmosphere that fosters learning. Students feel they can make comments and ask questions concerning the topics being discussed. As we are working with the three components — **separate, simplify,** and **facilitate** — we are also using additional teaching strategies. For instance, when we **separate** in our teaching, we are also asking students to act upon movement directions. We ask students to react or "act upon" a direction that is given visually, verbally, or by using hands-on guidance; for example, a classroom teacher might ask a student to walk to the office to get a form.

Teaching Guidelines

Keep the following guidelines in mind as you go through the day asking students to act upon movement directions:

1. Remember to *separate* — use only one presentation method at a time. Either demonstrate, use verbal directions, or use hands-on guidance.
2. When possible, simplify by using static movements — that is, pause after each single movement for ease of copying. Static movements are easier for beginners to follow than are dynamic (continuous) movements, which must be continually tracked by the follower. Regular-speed movements are sometimes hard for students to see in detail. Therefore, when possible, use static movements or try to slow the actions to a slow dynamic movement.
3. In giving verbal directions, keep the number of words to a minimum — pause after each direction is given so the student can process and respond to what has been said.
4. Keep the movements simple — older students do not necessarily require more difficult movements. When you are keeping the movements at a basic level, you are setting the stage for all students to be successful.
5. Make the movements age-appropriate — for example, older students respond better to off-the-body movements such as swinging the arms, punching in the air, or shaking the hands in front of the body or between the legs, whereas younger students are more successful with movements such as patting knees with hands or tapping knees with elbows.
6. Encourage students to assume leadership — give students opportunities to be the leader for the entire class, for small groups, and for their partners. We can learn a great deal about our students when we observe them as they take on a leadership role.

What is Static Movement and Dynamic Movement?

Static movement — This is a movement that stops or pauses before a new movement is presented. For example, students copy the teacher as she puts her arms straight out in front of her body. The teacher looks around the room to make sure students have their hands out in front of them before she does another movement. To give another example, students copy as the teacher pauses to show the relationship of the legs to the arms in an overhand throw.

Dynamic movement — This is a movement that continues without pausing, for example, the teacher has her hands on her hips and begins to move both hands slowly until both hands are above her head with arms straight. As another example, a teacher demonstrates dribbling a basketball; her hand continues to move up and down as the ball goes up and down. Other examples of dynamic movement include walking and typing on a computer.

Describing Movement

It is also useful to ask students to describe movement throughout the day. This is especially helpful when we are using the **facilitate** component of the teaching model. It is important to have students talk about and describe what they are doing with their bodies when working on concepts and skills. This use of language as the body is moving helps build **cognitive-motor links.** A cognitive-motor link is a group of connected thought processes associated with a motor task. As students begin doing sports and having other skill-related experiences in their lives, they must call on a wide range of cognitive-motor links developed through previous experiences.

For example, a hockey goalie tries to predict the direction of a shot by searching for perceptual clues that provide advance information, then moves into position. The figure skater about to perform a triple axel jump followed immediately by a triple toe loop must prepare for this combined action with the flexibility in mind to change the plan if something goes wrong. Imagine a 16-year-old driving the car when a deer runs out in front of him. He must react appropriately or

For this activity, students talk about their movements as they are doing them.

lose control of the car. All of these are examples of decision-making processes that involve the anticipation, planning, regulation, and interpretation of motor performance. They are only possible because the individual has already developed a bank of cognitive-motor links that enable him or her to coordinate quick thinking with precise actions.

Having students describe their movements is one strategy that must be used each day to help students develop the skills needed to make quick decisions when life calls on them to quickly process information and react physically.

Below are five strategies we can use to support students when we are asking them to describe movement.

1. Provide language by commenting on movements students are performing. Students need to hear descriptive language for their movements. This allows teachers to introduce new words students might not know. Hearing that word as they are doing the movement helps the students to make a cognitive-motor link.
2. Encourage students to talk about the movement while they are in motion. Allow students to talk out loud or work with a partner, and have the students describe their actions as they are performing the movement.
3. Engage students by asking them to think about and describe how they plan to move or how they plan to accomplish a concept or skill.
4. Allow time for students to talk about their movements after the movements are completed.
5. Ask students to use **learner SAY & DO.** This strategy requires students to link each single movement to a single descriptive word. This allows thought to direct the movement and unites action, thought, and language. For example, a student using **learner SAY & DO** is marching and swinging his arms. Each time one foot touches the ground the student says the

word MARCH, directing intention to his leg movements; his arms swing without conscious intention but, rather, through muscle memory (see p. 29). Another example of **learner SAY & DO** is when a student tosses and catches a ball. Each time the student tosses the ball he says, **TOSS,** and when he catches the ball, he says, **CATCH.** (See Chapter 3 for two related strategies, **learner WHISPER & DO** and **learner SAY & DO.**)

Summary

Now that you have read this chapter, you can use the strategies described to get your students engaged in learning! Using the components of the ETM teaching model allows us to **separate** information and **simplify** skills so all students can be successful. In the **facilitate** component of the teaching model, teachers deepen students' understanding by asking divergent (open-ended) questions. This strategy also builds stronger bonds between student and teacher and engages students in conversation. Two other important strategies that help get students involved are encouraging students to act upon movement directions and encouraging students to describe movement.

In the next chapter we will take a close look at particular ways we move our bodies and specific strategies for helping children learn these movements. This discussion will guide you further in applying the **separate, simplify,** and **facilitate** components of the teaching model introduced in this chapter.

This student is using learner SAY & DO while moving on and off her fitness step.

A student explores different ways of striking the birdie with his racket.

3
Ways We Move Our Bodies

Purposeful movement requires conscious thought on the part of the student. It is planned beforehand; it is accompanied by thought; it can be recalled and discussed.

— Phyllis S. Weikart

Types of Movement

We use two terms to categorize the way we move our bodies: **gross motor (large muscle)** and **fine motor (small muscle).** To further define the movements belonging to these two categories, we use the terms **locomotor movement** and **nonlocomotor movement.** Locomotor movement can be defined as nonanchored movement consisting of transfers of weight in personal or general space. All traveling movements are locomotor movements, for example, running, walking, and hopping. In addition, movements such as jogging in place, jumping rope, and stepping in place are considered to be locomotor movements because they, too, require weight transfers.

Students practice locomotor movements in the classroom.

Moving their hands on and off their body is one nonlocomotor movement students perform in this classroom.

Nonlocomotor movement involves moving while a body part is anchored — for example, shaking one's hands, swinging one's arms, or touching one's toes. Locomotor and nonlocomotor movements are more difficult when they are combined together (called **integrated movement**) or when we add an object (called **moving with objects**). Examples of integrated movement include performing jumping jacks, dribbling a basketball while running, or playing a musical instrument while marching in the band (note that the last two examples also involve objects). Moving with objects can be more difficult than simple locomotor and nonlocomotor movement because the use of objects often involves timing — either one's own timing or the timing of a group or leader. When moving with an object, the object can become an extension of one's arm, for example, when swinging a tennis racket or a baseball bat.

It is very important when working with students that we encourage them to use **purposeful movement** (e.g., movement that requires conscious thought and is planned beforehand). For example, in the *Education Through Movement (ETM)* teaching model, we constantly ask students to describe and act upon movement directions. Having students think about and label their movements leads to those movements becoming planned and purposeful. In this chapter we are going to discuss locomotor movement, nonlocomotor movement, fine-motor movement, integrated movement, and movement with objects. We will examine each area of movement separately, but keep in mind that students are developing skills in these areas simultaneously. At the end of the chapter we'll discuss the format of the activities in Chapters 4 and 5.

Locomotor Movement

Students' early **locomotor movements** include rolling, crawling, and walking. Developing the basic skills involved with locomotor movement is a gradual process.

In the previous chapter we talked about how important it is to progress from simple to more complex movements when working on movement concepts with students. This principle applies to all levels of motor evelopment. s

LOCOMOTOR MOVEMENT

This chart presents the basic locomotor movements (movements with weight transfers) showing the progression from the simplest to the most complex movements.

SIMPLE → MORE COMPLEX

Alternating single movements
Examples include crawling, walking, marching, galloping, sliding (sideward gallop). Skipping is an example of an alternating locomotor movement that is more complex.

Two-sided movements
Example: jumping

One side...other side movements
For example, a student hops on one foot for several repetitions and then hops on the other foot for several repetitions.

The simplest type of locomotor movement is called **alternating,** and it requires transfer of weight from one foot immediately to the other foot. An example of a **single alternating locomotor movement** is marching. You can use the strategy learner SAY & DO (see pp. 16–17) with a single alternating movement: for example, saying the word MARCH each time weight is transferred from one foot to the other (alternating). It is very important to give younger students, or students with limited motor experiences, plenty of time to explore single alternating locomotor movements such as walking, running, galloping, sliding, and marching. Students need to try these movements in various directions and at different levels, for example, when a student walks backward with his body stretched up high.

Skipping is also considered an alternating locomotor movement but it is more complex because it combines two different weight transfers. A student must move from one foot to the other foot (step), and from one foot to the same foot (hop). Sometimes we as teachers try to break down the skill of skipping by using the words STEP, HOP. We tend to encourage students to slow the movement down, which actually changes the timing of skipping. Skipping has an uneven timing — it is the same timing that we see and feel when we gallop or slide (sideward gallop). It is important when students are working on skipping that they keep the movement uneven. To help students with their skipping, you might encourage them to gallop and make sure they are switching feet to alternate which foot is the lead foot. Another strategy would be to encourage students to hop on one foot several times and then hop on the other foot several times. This will help them develop the leg strength needed for skipping. These two strategies help students to develop strength and balance in their legs.

Jumping is a movement that uses two sides of the body at the same time and is considered more difficult than alternating locomotor movements such as **walking** or **galloping.** Jumping requires students to have strength in their legs as well as balance, coordination, and timing. Jumping involves taking off with two feet and landing on two feet, or jumping from one foot and landing on two. A jump is defined by the landing, not the takeoff. Some students have problems getting their feet off the floor because they do not have the strength in their legs to propel them-

One of the simplest single alternating locomotor movements is marching.

selves far enough upward. It is important that you provide opportunities in your classroom for students to explore jumping. This can be done by having objects or props available for students to jump off or jump over.

The hardest locomotor movement is the **hop.** Hopping requires more strength, balance, coordination, and basic timing than does jumping because of the one-foot takeoff and same-foot landing. It is important to remember that all the locomotor movements are developed in conjunction with each other and not in isolation. In other words, students do not learn how to walk and gallop, then learn how to jump, and finally learn how to hop. Students are developing these skills simultaneously, but we as teachers need to keep in mind the simple-to-complex order of skill development when working with students. It is very important to have students "play" with the various locomotor move-

Jumping involves taking off with two feet and landing on two feet, or jumping from one foot and landing on two.

ments. As we discussed in Chapter 2, "Getting Students Involved," it is also imperative that we get students to move with purpose — that is, to plan movements, to act upon movement directions, and, finally, to describe and discuss their movements with others.

Nonlocomotor Movement

The second category we use to describe the way students move is called **nonlocomotor movement.** This can be defined as movements students can do in personal space with a body part anchored in some way. Weight is not transferred when students are doing nonlocomotor movement. For example, a student can swing both arms while her feet are anchored to the ground, or a student can "ride a bicycle" while lying on the ground with his back anchored to the ground and his feet in the air. Students can find many ways to use nonlocomotor movement while standing or while seated.

NONLOCOMOTOR MOVEMENT

This chart presents the basic nonlocomotor movements (movements without weight transfers), showing the progression from the simplest to the most complex movements.

SIMPLE → MORE COMPLEX

Two sides, symmetrical movements

- **Action words —** Single words students use to describe their movements;
  Examples: pound, shake, wiggling thumbs and fingers
- **Basic movements**
  Examples: twist, swing, turn, rock
- **Sequenced movements**
  Examples: bend/straighten, push/pull, open/close

One side...other side movements
Example: swinging one arm several times and then swinging the other arm, holding the first arm still

Alternating movements
Example: swinging arms back and forth while one arm is forward, the other arm is back

---

Let's take a closer look at nonlocomotor movements, from simple to more complex. The simplest nonlocomotor movements are movements done with both sides of the body at the same time. Examples might include a student using both hands at the same time to pat his knees, or a student shaking both hands at the same time in front of her body. When students are given the opportunity to explore nonlocomotor movements, they come up with many different movements. One of the strategies we use with students is to ask them to label their movements with learner SAY & DO, a strategy that allows students to create cognitive-motor links — a group of connected thought processes associated with a motor task (see p. 15). When students give a name or a word to an action, we call that an **action word.** Action words that students might use include *pound, shake, wiggle, punch, flick, flap, slash, dab, snap, press,* and *tap.* An action word may be any word a student gives you for his nonlocomotor movement.

According to Phyllis S. Weikart, there are 12 basic nonlocomotor movements. Those movements are bend, straighten, twist, turn, swing, rock, push, pull, curl, stretch, rise, and fall. Remember to model even the simplest movements. For example, if you want the students to swing their arms, make sure you model swinging both arms at the same time, symmetrically, because two-sided movements are easier than alternating movements (this is unlike the case in locomotor movement, in which alternating movements are simpler). Allow students to explore and share their own way of swinging their arms. They will likely come up with some of the more difficult movements that you also want them to experience. If no one shares a movement that you had in mind, show the movement using *visual separating* (this strategy is discussed on p. 10). When using learner SAY & DO, it is easier for students to do one movement and use one single word; for example, when students turn their arms and say the word TURN each time their arms rotate. A task that is a little more difficult for students is a **sequenced movement.** This is a movement that has two parts, with one movement followed by another; for example, *bend/ straighten.* In this example, students may use both arms to show bending and straightening. If you put words to this movement, make sure the words match the movements you are doing.

More complex nonlocomotor movements include using one side of the body in repetition and then using the other side. An example of this is twisting one arm in front several times while holding the other arm still, then switching and twisting the opposite arm while holding the other arm still. Younger students have a very hard time holding one body part still while moving the other. This type of movement begins to set students up for the most difficult of the nonlocomotor movements: alternating movements. In alternating nonlocomotor movement, one alternates movement of a specific body part with another part. For example, when a student is punching in the air, he punches with one hand, followed immediately by the other hand.

Why Is It Important to Learn About Movement and Motor Development?

Whether you are a physical educator teaching the golf swing, or a kindergarten teacher showing your students how to hold the pencil correctly to write, it is important to know the categories of movement and motor-development sequences. When you are working with a class of 25–30 students and some students are having trouble mastering a skill, this information will give you an idea of how to help them. You need to know how to break down locomotor or nonlocomotor movements to help students find a way to be successful as they move in a purposeful way.

As mentioned earlier, all movements are made up of either locomotor or nonlocomotor movements. There are several other terms that describe particular movements in a more specific way, but they all still pertain to locomotor and nonlocomotor movements. Next we will discuss these terms and take a look at what they describe.

Fine-Motor Movement

Fine-motor movement is very important to students' success in their everyday lives. This type of movement requires a high degree of control and precision and generally involves small movements of the hands, wrists, fingers, feet, toes, lips, and tongue. At a very early age we expect students to cut with scissors; zip their coats; tie their shoes; write or color with pencils, crayons, or markers; and do many other tasks. If you take a moment and think in detail about the movements required for any one of these tasks, you can understand why youngsters need time and practice to master these skills.

Many times our focus as adults is on the task rather than the movement(s) required to complete it. If you have ever taught kindergarten students — and it doesn't matter whether you are a classroom teacher or a physical education teacher — you have experienced this situation. Take the example of a kindergarten student who comes into your classroom with her shoes untied. We all have developed strategies over the years to deal with this scenario, but have we ever resolved the underlying situation? We may have found ourselves asking another student in the class to tie the student's shoe, we may have tied the shoe ourselves, or perhaps we told the student to put the shoestrings in his shoe. Sound familiar?

A student uses fine-motor skills as he writes for an assignment in his science class.

Reflecting back on our discussion of nonlocomotor movement (see pp. 24–25), what must be in place for the student to successfully tie her shoe? We can visualize the movements required to complete the task: the student must hold one hand still while using the other hand to manipulate the shoestring over, around, and under the hand that is being held still. Then the student must pull the string through a loop she made. If the student has not had all the simple movement experiences discussed in the nonlocomotor movement section, and if the student has not been asked to describe those movements, it is very difficult for the student to understand and perform a fine-motor movement such as this. Fine-motor movements are difficult because they are composed of such small movements and therefore require true body awareness. Another example is zipping and unzipping a coat. Students have to put the zipper together and then pull the zipper tab up or down with one hand while holding the coat edge with the other hand. Students have to have an understanding of direction to complete this task. In sum, students must have many and varied experiences with nonlocomotor movement before they can successfully complete fine-motor tasks. As adults with a great deal of experience with these tasks, we can forget how many movements and skills are required to complete these tasks until we break them down.

Integrated Movement

When students move two or more different areas of the body together purposefully at the same time, they are engaging in **integrated movement.** Examples of integrated movement include marching in place while bending and straightening the arms, performing jumping jacks, marching to music while clapping hands to the beat of the music, and marching while playing an instrument.

Using both arms and legs to jump through the hoop, this student demonstrates integrated movement.

Integrated movement can be performed in any position. For example, students who are lying down can carry out exercises in which their arms and legs are synchronized. Likewise, if they are seated, they can move their arms, trunk, and head together purposefully. Almost all sports skills involve integrated movements performed in a wide variety of combinations using arms and legs at the same time.

Integrated movements require thoughtful, conscious effort and involve exactness and precise coordination. Because these movements are so exacting, students should not be expected to perform them with mastery until second grade. Some students who have had many natural play experiences may be ready before this age, but most students are not yet sufficiently mature in their motor development to be successful. Students tend to be more adept with integrated movement after they have moved from the preoperational stage (occurs between the ages of 2 and 6) to the concrete operational stage of development (7–11 years of age). See the sidebar, right, for definitions of these stages. A student who is in the concrete operational stage is ready to follow rules, and most of the skills in sports require correctness and a rule or guideline

Stages of Development

The four stages of human development identified by Jean Piaget (1969) are at the sensorimotor, preoperational, concrete operational, and formal operational stages.

The sensorimotor stage occurs from birth to about age 2 in typically developing children. This is a time when children explore the world through movement and their five senses. During this time children are generally self-focused, or egocentric.

The preoperational stage occurs between the ages of 2 and 6, and is characterized by language development. Children at this stage are not yet capable of concrete logic and still have difficulty seeing others' points of view. During this stage children become increasingly able to use symbols, which is seen in the increase in pretend play.

The concrete operational stage takes place between the ages of 7 and 11. During this stage children begin thinking more logically about concrete events but still have difficulty understanding abstract or hypothetical concepts. They are more and more able to see others' points of view.

The formal operational stage permits older children and adults to take in information, make observations and hypotheses, test their hypotheses, and use deductive logic to solve problems. These skills are considered part of "abstract thinking."

This student is inhibiting his left side while dribbling a basketball with his right hand.

to help make them successful. For example, in basketball a player must dribble a basketball with only one hand on the ball at a time and keep her head up so she can see where she is going.

For students to be able to successfully use integrated movement, they need to have mastered the following:

The ability to inhibit movement: Students need to be able to hold one side still while the other side is moving. Dribbling a basketball with one hand is an example of this ability. You have to hold one hand still while you strike (dribble) the ball with the other hand.

The ability to combine two concepts: Students need to be able to do two different things at the same time. An example of this would be jumping jacks (jumping with legs and feet moving apart and then together again while extending the arms up and down).

Strategies for Teaching Integrated Movement

As you begin to work with your students using integrated movement, it is important to use two key strategies: **layering** and **learner SAY & DO.** Below we'll use jumping jacks as an example to show how to apply these two strategies.

Layering. Imagine that you have students start a movement sequence using their legs and then add the movement sequence of the arms to it. Do not stop and teach the arm movements separately. For example, to teach jumping jacks, have students start by using only their legs. First, the students jump with feet apart, then with feet together. After doing this sequence of leg movements several times, have students "layer on" the arm movements without stopping the legs. This strategy is effective because nonlocomotor (anchored) movements (in this case, those with the arms) are usually easier than locomotor movements and can easily be added once the locomotor movements have been practiced. Layering is useful when establishing aerobic routines that use arms and legs together.

Learner SAY & DO. This strategy involves students' labeling a movement with a single word and speaking that label as they do the movement. In the example above (jumping jacks) students are moving their feet apart and then together. The words APART, TOGETHER would be the labels for this sequence. Students practice these leg movements and speak the words to match what their bodies are doing. Once students are secure with the leg pattern, the teacher presents the arm movements visually. Students copy the movement and then practice them without the legs, continuing to speak the same words used for the legs: APART, TOGETHER. When students have mastered the arm movements, their next step is to unite the two areas of the body in movement. Students SAY & DO the leg movements (APART, TOGETHER), integrating them with the arm movements. This integrated movement pattern is repeated until it is stored in "muscle memory," that is, until students can do the movement without having to think about it. Using the learner SAY & DO strategy allows students to establish a cognitive relationship between the arm and leg movements. As this relationship becomes stronger and students are able to perform the movements better, students can progress to whispering the words **(WHISPER & DO)**, and eventually, to thinking the words to themselves as they perform the movements **(THINK & DO)**. Further practice leads to muscle memory (doing without thinking).

The Four-Step Language Process

Step 1: SAY — The student uses simple language to describe the movement; usually one word.

Step 2: SAY & DO — The student says the word while doing the movement. For example, when the student is marching, he or she says the word MARCH with each step.

Step 3: WHISPER & DO — This step is the same as Step 2 except the student whispers the word rather than speaking the word out loud.

Step 4: THINK & DO — In this step, the student thinks the word rather than speaking or whispering.

— From *Teaching Movement & Dance,* 6th ed., p. 28

Moving With Objects

The term **moving with objects** applies to the basic manipulative skills of sports and games. Students also use objects when they are cutting paper, writing, coloring, sorting small objects, or playing handheld musical instruments. While these activities may at first seem unrelated, many of the same teaching principles apply since all involve the use of handheld objects and require students to develop timing skills.

Exploration

Exploration is a key principle to remember in activities that involve objects. When we use objects, we are almost always looking for a specific skill to be mastered. We want the students to use a pencil to make a well-written letter, word, or sentence; to play a melody on the recorder; to learn the correct way to dribble a basketball, swing a golf club, or throw a ball. However, it is important for students to have opportunities to explore objects and think of their own ways to use them before the skill is introduced. Students' explorations with objects can provide time for the teacher to observe and evaluate their various levels of motor development.

The teacher's comments during the students' exploration can serve to acknowledge students' ideas and also give others ideas to explore. Asking a student to think of another way to try some-

This student uses both hands to move small objects during math class.

thing may also expand creativity. It is also important during this exploratory phase to ask students to try to use the object with the opposite hand or foot. Even though most students in grades K–5 have determined their hand and foot preference, it is still very important to have them explore using the object with the other side of the body. This allows students to engage both sides of the brain as well as to work on coordination of body parts.

Students' explorations with objects can provide time for teachers to observe and evaluate students' varying levels of motor development. For example, suppose a female student is using a soccer ball to explore dribbling, and you notice she can handle the ball very well. In this case, you might ask the student to tell you how she is dribbling the soccer ball and how she is able to control the ball so well. The student may share information about how her father is a soccer coach and how she has been going to soccer camps and practicing since she was three years old. This student is going to be much more skilled than the other students because of her experiences. Ask yourself how you are going to meet her needs and keep her progressing to a higher skill level.

This student explores using his body to make scarves move in various ways.

Exploring with objects. When students are working with objects, be sure to have the students use the learner SAY & DO strategy discussed earlier in this chapter. Encouraging students to add words to organize the movements allows them to develop timing in working with the object. After students have had time to explore movements and identify appropriate words to use with them, you will want to have the students put the object down and try doing the movement without the object. This allows students the opportunity to concentrate on the movements needed to attain the skill you are working to develop. For example, you might do the following if you are working on the skills *toss and catch:* Have the students put the balls down and pretend to toss the balls up with their hands while saying the word TOSS, and then have the students pretend to catch the balls and say the word CATCH. Allowing the students to try this movement without the ball gives them the opportunity to work on tracking up and down without having to think about actually catching the balls. I use the learner SAY & DO strategy all the time with my middle-school basketball team. Sometimes just taking the basketball out of their hands and having them practice the movement and say the words makes all the difference in their understanding of the particular skill we are trying to improve.

By putting her rope down to practice jumping, this student is able to concentrate on the movements needed for rope jumping.

Another important point to remember before allowing students to work with objects is to provide objects that are the correct size for the group that is going to be handling them. If you have scarves or ribbon wands, be sure they are small enough or large enough for students to use. For example, the ribbon wands that have a long ribbon tail are not suitable for small kindergarten students. You should use ribbon wands that are shorter in length. (A good rule of thumb is to keep the ribbons shorter than the length of the average child's arm so that children do not step on them.) Similarly, in selecting jump ropes, be sure you have many and varied lengths of ropes to accommodate students. It is also vital to have enough objects (e.g., beanbags, lummi sticks, paper plates, scarves) so students can have an object for each hand. It is also important to plan your class times so students have as much time as possible to actively work with the objects. Try to avoid situations in which students are standing in line and waiting for a turn. If we provide enough objects for each student, and we allow time for exploration, all students can be busy using their own object in their own space.

In discussing movement with objects, we have touched on timing and creativity several times. In my experience, students tend to be more creative when they are using objects rather than when moving without them. In addition, I know from my own childhood experiences that students may feel less self-conscious when moving with objects. I recall as a child I often felt more comfortable when I had an object in my hand because I felt like people were watching the object more than they were watching me. Your students may feel the same way.

As for timing, movement with objects almost always includes timing — either one's own timing or the timing of a group or leader. The addition of an object increases the level of difficulty when students are performing movements or trying to develop skills in a "timed way." Not

These students, who are small, have shorter handles for holding on to their ribbon wands. Also, the teachers have made sure the ribbons are no longer than the length of the students' bodies.

only do the students have to think about the movement and the timing, but they also have to think about manipulating the object. An example of a student using an object with her own timing might be when the student is bouncing a ball every time she says the word BOUNCE. The student would be following the timing of a leader if she were bouncing the ball every time the leader said BOUNCE. For some students it is very difficult to keep a movement going in the timing of another person.

Movement Extensions

Now, let's take a deeper look at the movement extensions — **creative movement** and **basic timing.** Creative movement and basic timing extend students' abilities to reach another level of understanding and skill performance. We will examine each extension separately.

Creative Movement

Creative movement can be such a free, fun, and individual experience for students. By *creative movement* we mean taking a familiar movement and changing it in some way. However, some students are not comfortable developing their own ideas, so it is important to set up a classroom climate that encourages creativity and respect for everyone's ideas. As much as possible, plan and structure activities so students are less likely to become self-conscious as they express their ideas. The suggestions in the list below will help.

Creative movement cannot be taught at a specific time or place. Instead, it develops over time as teachers promote and support students' ideas. Here are a few essential ingredients that Phyllis S. Weikart has said are needed to create an environment that encourages creativity:

- Supportive teachers and peers who recognize students for their creative efforts
- An absence of judgmental comments that lead students to compare themselves with one another or try to be "correct"
- An absence of demonstrations that might imply that there is only one way to approach a problem
- Opportunities for students to begin creative efforts by imitating others and gradually branching out to suggesting original ideas
- Opportunities for students to interact and share by working in pairs or small groups
- Adult support in the form of techniques and suggestions that are age-appropriate and make students feel they are not being observed

(Weikart, 2006, p. 57)

A common theme runs through many of the items in this list: first and foremost, be supportive of all students' efforts. It is important to avoid statements that compare one student's movements to another. For example, saying to a student "I like the way you are moving around the room" may be intended as a positive strategy, but it can imply that other students are not doing the action correctly or that you don't like *their* ideas.

Avoid judging students, and try to structure activities so students feel free to be creative. For instance, try giving students verbal directions rather than demonstrating the movements — this gives students a chance to develop their own movements rather than copying the teacher's. It also allows each student to respond to the verbal directions in his or her own way. Another way to support creativity is to allow students the opportunity to work in their own space (personal space) rather than in a particular formation, such as a circle. When students work in a circle, where they can see one another, they are sometimes hesitant to try new ideas. They feel more "hidden" if they are spread out around the room or play area and so may feel more comfortable experimenting with movements.

You can also encourage creativity by planning activities around **problem solving** and **representation.** Problem solving allows students to finish or complete a movement direction. For example, students may be asked to swing their arms. In this instance, the teacher has identified the movement and the body parts that students are to use, but it is up to the students to choose how and where they will swing their arms. Representation, a related strategy, involves using movement as a creative medium to reenact familiar actions or happenings. For example, students might be asked to move in a "bumpy" way. This suggestion fosters creativity because it asks students to use an idea with which they are familiar, in a completely new context. The teacher's role is not only to support but also to extend students' representations (in this case, of what "bumpy" looks like) by asking them questions that call attention to how their bodies are moving.

Choreography is another way to experience creative movement with students. Choreography is developed by taking movement patterns and sequencing them to music. Allow students to explore and create movements to music to make up dances and routines. For students to be successful with choreography, they need to have skill with locomotor and nonlocomotor movements. They also have to be comfortable with integrated movement, and they have to have basic timing. So this brings us to the second movement extension — basic timing.

Students explore and create movement sequences for a choreographed routine to a musical recording.

Basic Timing (Steady Beat)

Basic timing, defined by Phyllis S. Weikart in her book *Teaching Movement & Dance,* 6th ed., is the ability to independently feel, express, and keep the underlying steady beat of a rhyme, song, or recorded/live musical selection with nonlocomotor and locomotor movement (Weikart, 2006, p. 463). Weikart has concluded that steady beat is central to almost everything we do and that mastery of it has lifelong significance. In my work with the *Education Through Movement* program since 1993, I have found there is reason for us as educators to pay attention to this skill that so many take for granted.

According to Weikart, students develop basic timing in two stages. The first stage is **beat awareness.** We all have a natural, internal steady beat. Some of us have a faster internal beat than others. Beat awareness involves mastering three abilities: keeping your own internal beat, matching an external steady beat that is spoken or shown by someone using verbal or visual directions, and performing nonlocomotor or locomotor movements to a rhyme, song, or recording selection. In the *Education Through Movement* program, we encourage students and teachers to move in steady beat using two related beats. Dr. Edwin Gordon, a music theorist, has developed two terms that describe these beats: **microbeat** and **macrobeat.** For the purpose of this book, we will define *microbeat* as each beat in a group of two or three beats. When we refer to a "microbeat movement," we mean the movement is done on each beat of the music. *Macrobeat* is defined as the accented first beat in a group of two or three beats. A "macrobeat movement" is done on the strong, or accented, beat.

Earlier in this book we discussed using the strategy learner SAY & DO. An example of this strategy is a student performing a movement such as walking and saying the word WALK each time one of his feet touches the floor. This student demonstrates beat awareness by moving to his own internal steady beat. Students are also using beat awareness when a movement matches a steady movement that is spoken verbally. Another example of beat awareness using the macro-beat would be a student patting his knees with both hands on the macrobeat. For example, the student would say KNEES each time his hands landed on his knees. The student is patting the knees to a beat that is approximate to a natural rocking movement, or the tempo at which you might rock an infant. This creates a 2 to 1 relationship between the microbeat (walking tempo) and the macrobeat (rocking tempo).

Beat competence is the second stage of basic timing development that Weikart describes. This means being able to independently identify (feel), express, and keep the microbeat or macrobeat while using nonlocomotor or locomotor movement to a rhyme, song, or recording. Students need many experiences with nonlocomotor movement to the rocking beat (macrobeat) to feel the organization of rhymes, songs, and recordings. Students also need time to experience the feel of the walking beat (microbeat).

You can use the strategies on page 36 with students during the beat competence stage as you are working toward helping them develop basic timing.

Feeling the beat of the music is one of the things these students are learning as they march to a musical recording.

Basic Timing — Developmental Sequence

Nonlocomotor Movement	Macrobeat* →	Microbeat* →	Either
Locomotor Movement	Microbeat →	Macrobeat →	Either

Grade	Timing
Preschool and Kindergarten	Nonlocomotor movement in macrobeat Locomotor movement in microbeat
Grade 1	Nonlocomotor movement in macrobeat and microbeat Locomotor movement in microbeat
Grade 2	Nonlocomotor movement in macrobeat and microbeat Locomotor movement in microbeat and macrobeat
Grade 3	Extending timing to all learning areas, which includes singing and moving, performing accurate rhythm patterns, and integrating movement sequences from a solid foundation in steady beat.

**Macrobeat* and *microbeat* are Dr. Edwin Gordon's terms.
(From *Teaching Movement & Dance,* by Phyllis S. Weikart, p. 65)

Ways to Help Students Develop Beat Competence

Provide opportunities for students to

1. Use nonlocomotor movement to keep the steady beat. For example, have students swing both arms or rock to the steady beat (macrobeat, or rocking tempo) to a rhyme, song, or musical recording.
2. Use locomotor movement to keep the steady beat. For example, have students march to every beat of the music (microbeat) in personal space.
3. Be the leader and keep steady beat while other students copy the movement and timing of the leader's steady beat.
4. Listen to a word spoken repeatedly and match the steady beat (learner SAY & DO). For example, each time a student hears the word TWIST, he twists both arms.

Strategies to use with students when working on steady beat:

1. When doing movements to rhymes and songs, have students start the movement first, then add the rhyme or song.
2. Use instrumental recordings (vocals can be distracting and pull students off task). With songs that are sung by the teacher in the classroom, you can take out words and sing the melody on a neutral syllable such as "bah."
3. Have students do their movements quietly or silently so that those who cannot yet keep a steady beat don't pull other students off their beat. Remember that pats and taps should be silent.
4. Encourage students to choose their own movement to keep steady beat (e.g., marching, twisting the arms, patting toes).

Strategies for helping "untimed" students in your class:

1. Encourage the student to set the beat by showing a movement with his own tempo.
2. Use tactile reinforcement of steady beat by patting the steady beat on top of the student's shoulders or rocking the student.

3. Place your hands under the student's hands as she is patting so your hands touch the student's legs. Your patting will model the beat for the student.
4. Rock with the entire class or smaller groups sitting close together (bodies touching).
5. When working in the groups, have each student try out the movement in his or her own timing first. Have students try the movement again with a partner, then in small or large groups, before adding the song or instrumental recording.

Benefits of Steady Beat

Over the years, classroom teachers have found that using steady beat in their class each and every day helps students to refocus on their school work. Students who have the ability to maintain a steady beat independently appear to be able to organize their thoughts and actions better than students who cannot keep a steady beat. Many teachers use the strategies listed above each time they are teaching new rhymes to students or are having students memorize information such as letters, multiplication facts, names of states, and so forth. Saying a rhyme while keeping a steady beat allows students to focus on the meaning of the words in the rhyme.

Steady Beat for Transitions

As you take breaks in your classroom schedule or are transitioning from one part of the day to another, try having the students get out of their seats as you put on an instrumental recording. Allow students to plan what movements they would like to do to the beat of the music. By using steady beat in different ways, students develop basic timing skills; as they develop these skills, you will observe greater fluency in the students' speech and reading.

In physical education classes and sports, basic timing is very important. All sports skills require timing and coordination. A student must perform a sequence of steady movements, not only alone but in time with others. Consider, for example, a hockey game in which a student is taking the puck down the ice and is looking for a way to score. His teammates are skating down, trying to anticipate his timing so that they are in position to receive a pass. In football, a quarterback making a pass has to anticipate where the receiver will be so he can throw the ball where the receiver can catch it. For students to develop basic timing, they need many experiences using nonlocomotor and locomotor movements. They need to work with a partner to try to match the other person's steady movement; they need to be able to move in creative ways to music; and, most important, they need time to explore, plan, and discuss movements — that is, they need to be able to discover movements and their own timing before we take them on to skill development. Teachers tend to hurry the process of discovery because they want perfection or mastery far too quickly. We must remember the maxim that "to do is to understand"; students' mastery of skills will come much more quickly when they have a deeper understanding of the basic concepts.

The Activities in This Book

Now you are ready to use the activities, which are in the next two chapters of this book. As you do so, you may wish to review Chapters 1–3. The activities in Chapters 4 and 5 are meant to supplement your existing curriculum, and each is designed to teach exploration in a particular concept area.

Activities. In Chapter 4, you'll find movement activities for grades K–2, and in Chapter 5, movement activities for grades 3–5. These activities were written using the teaching strategies and developmental information presented in Chapters 1–3. Each activity contains the following elements:

By asking an "essential question" about the activity's movement concept at the beginning of the activity, the teacher focuses students' attention and gains an understanding of what they know.

- **Grade level:** Activities are clearly labeled in the top left-hand corner with either K–2 or 3–5.
- **Classroom symbol:** This symbol identifies those activities that can be done by a physical education teacher or a classroom teacher in his or her classroom, as contrasted with activities that require a larger space, such as a gym or playground.
- **Curriculum concepts:** These are the movement concepts targeted by the activity.
- **Physical Education National Standards:** These are the standards that the activity meets.
- **Description:** A brief description of the activity is given in italics.
- **Essential Questions:** These are the key questions related to the topic of the activity (e.g., "What are words we use to describe shapes that we make with our bodies?"). Many of the questions are basic, but they are very important. Asking the question at the beginning of class allows you to evaluate where your students are functioning at that particular moment. They will help you ask yourself, "What do my students know about the topic they are going to be working on today?"
- **Materials:** Each activity also lists materials that are needed.
- **Steps for Success:** These sections take you step-by-step through the activity.
- **Facilitation and reflection:** These sections contain prompts and questions to build on children's thinking and understanding.
- **Extensions:** These suggestions will give you ideas for follow-up activities. (*Note:* Some activities may not have extensions.)

- **More ideas for teachers:** Many of the dance activities in Chapter 5 include a section called "Lead-Up Activities," to help you prepare students for the main activity, and a section called "Teaching Suggestions" that will give you extra ideas for helping students to be successful.

❖ ❖ ❖

This book is not intended to provide you with a physical education curriculum. Rather, it offers strategies and information to promote active learning in your classroom, whether you are a physical education teacher or a classroom teacher. The activities in the book can help you experience joy and success in your teaching whether you are a first-year teacher or an experienced educator closing in on retirement. You will find information in this book that will help you create an enjoyable classroom environment in which students feel safe and free to be creative. Have fun exploring the activities with your students and remember, always plan to have students move with purpose!

Children need the opportunity to explore and think about movement before we consider skill development.

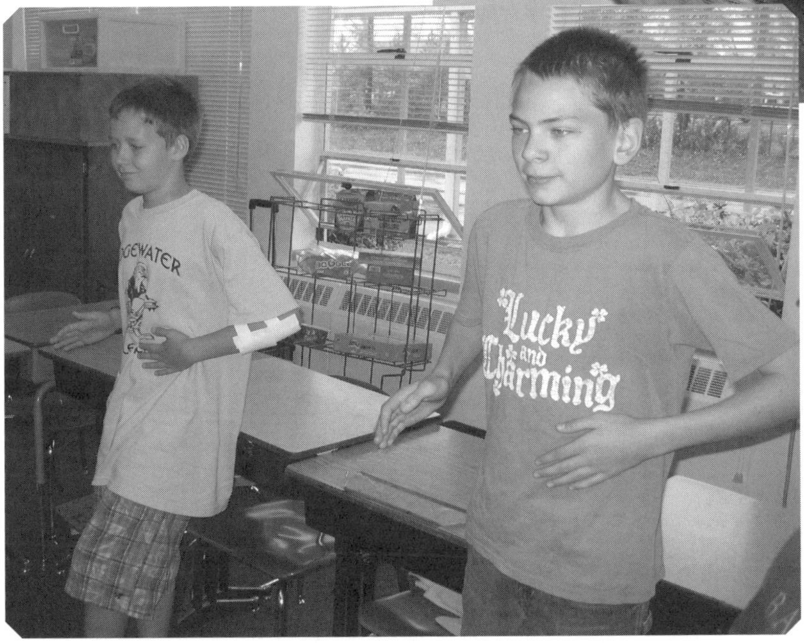

These students work together to develop a nonlocomotor movement sequence to music.

4
Activities for Grades K-2

1

Balance

In this activity students explore static and dynamic balance. Students will use balance puzzles to try out different positions to balance.

Essential Question

What does it mean to balance?

Curriculum Concepts

- Static balance
- Dynamic balance

Physical Education National Standard(s)

Standard 1

Materials

- Recording of "Seven Jumps" (on accompanying CD)
- Balance puzzles (Below is an example of a balance puzzle key. Balance puzzles are a visual representation of the body parts you want students to use to balance. The key gives the symbol and what they represent. If they see a picture of hands, then they put their hands on the floor to balance. If they see a picture of hands and head, then they do a balance with only their head and hands on the mat or floor.)

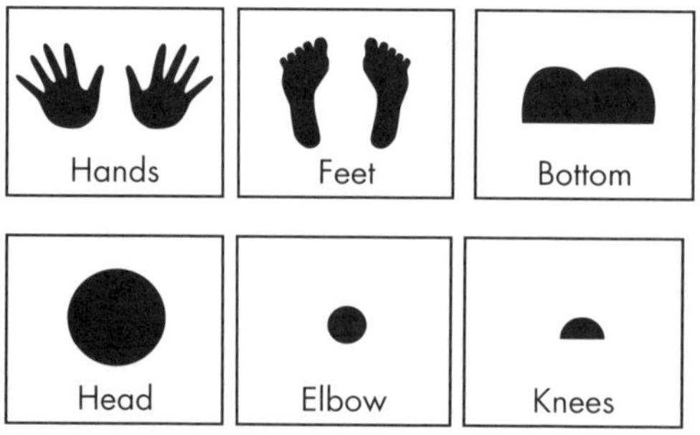

Terms for Weight Transfer Sequences

Static balance — This involves maintaining a desired shape in a stationary position. Examples might include handstands, headstands, and gymnastic balances.

Dynamic balance — This involves maintaining an on-balance position while moving, starting, and stopping. Example of a dynamic balance is running, skipping, and other locomotor movements.

Weight transfer — This involves taking weight from one body part and putting it on another.

Steps to Success

Step 1

Ask students the essential question "What does it mean to balance?" Discuss the difference between static balance (when you are not moving) and dynamic balance (when you are moving — this occurs with all locomotor movements). Ask students to look for static and dynamic balances during the warmup, which will occur in Step 3. (See definitions of static balance and dynamic balance on page 42.

Step 2

Ask students to explore balancing on different body parts. You might see one student standing on one foot with her arms straight over her head. Another student might decide to balance with one knee and two hands on the ground. You will observe many other ways the students try balancing during this exploration; comment on students' actions. For example, you might say, "I see that you are balancing on both knees and one hand."

Step 3

Lead a warmup to the recording of "Seven Jumps." During the warmup do dynamic balances (different locomotor movements) to the steady beat of the music and use many of the static balances during the pauses in the music.

Have students copy and identify (name) balances during the warmup, noticing dynamic balances as well as static balances and talking about which and how many body parts are touching the floor.

What Is Steady Beat?

Steady beat is the consistent, repetitive pulse that lies within every rhyme, song, or musical selection.

Step 4

After the warmup, ask students to recall some of the static and dynamic balances used during the warmup. Also ask how many of their body parts were touching the floor during the different balances.

Step 5

Have students explore ways they can balance while using different numbers of body parts. For example, Amir might balance on five body parts (one hand, two knees, and two feet). Students take turns sharing with the class, and the class copies each of the leaders. For example, Shelley shares a static balance with two body parts on the floor — she has her right hand and her right knee on the floor. Together with the other students, try Shelley's idea.

As this student explores a static balance, the teacher works with him as a partner as they determine how many body parts are used in the balance.

Step 6

Have students copy balance puzzles you show them.

Facilitation and Reflection

Ask students the following questions to help them reflect on their experiences and extend their thinking:

- *Which static balances are easier or harder?*
- *Which dynamic balances are easier or harder?*
- *What did you find out about balance?*
- *What are some of the differences between static and dynamic movement?*

Extensions

- Students can work in pairs and take turns being the leader and copying each other's static balance. The leader makes a static balance and the other person copies the balance. The person copying the balance tells the other person everything he can about the balance, including the body parts used during the balance.
- Students can work with a different partner to try out dynamic balances using the same procedure as above.

2

Batter, Batter, Swing

Students explore swinging a bat and experience hitting a stationary ball off a tee (cone).

Essential Question

What is a sideways swing when you have a bat in your hand?

Curriculum Concepts

- Manipulative skill — striking with a long implement
- Visual tracking
- Force

Physical Education National Standard(s)

Standard 1

Materials

- Plastic bats
- Balls (foam or plastic)
- Batting tees or cones
- Ball hanging from a rope or other type of line

  Note: You need to have enough equipment for each student.

Steps to Success

Step 1

Setting equipment up for the class:

- Set up an area where balls are attached to and hanging down from a rope or other type of line so students can reach them for striking. Make sure there is plenty of space between each ball so each child can swing a bat freely.
- Place tees and/or cones around the court (play space) with a ball.

Step 2

Ask students the essential question "What is a sideways swing?" Have the students get in personal space. Ask students to show how they would swing a baseball bat. Ask "What kind of swing are you using?"

Step 3

Give each student a plastic bat and have students explore hitting a hanging ball. Encourage students to swing at the hanging ball from each side of their body (right-handed and left-handed). Walk around and comment on what individual students are doing as they explore. This step is very important because it gives you real-time feedback about the abilities of the students.

Step 4

Ask for students to volunteer to share with the class how they were hitting the hanging ball. Have the rest of the class copy each leader. Ask questions or make comments, drawing attention to various aspects of the leader's swing. Start making students aware of how it is easier to hit the ball if you stand with your side facing the target (ball). Younger students may not be ready to stand sideways to hit the ball, so be sure to provide opportunities for other exploration.

Step 5

Have students (with a bat) go to a cone or tee. Have students explore how they would swing to hit a ball off the tee if a ball were to be placed there. (At this time the students are not using a ball.)

Step 6

Put a ball on a tee and ask students to watch you. Model for students how to measure how far away to stand from the ball. This is done by holding the bat and extending one's arms to the ball. Students will measure the distance they need to stand away from the tee to hit the ball with their arms and the bat extended. Have students swing the bat, hit the ball, and put the bat down beside the tee.

Have students retrieve the ball and get ready to hit again. Repeat the sequence. Allow students to repeat this sequence as many times as there is class time to do so.

Visual tracking and force are two of the concepts this student explores while learning to swing a bat.

Facilitation and Reflection

Ask students the following questions to help them reflect on their experiences and extend their thinking:

- *How do your hands grip the bat?*
- *Describe the "batting stance."*
- *What must you do to make contact with the ball?*

Extensions

Students find partners. One partner is the batter and the other partner tosses the ball for his or her partner to swing at. Be sure to use foam balls that will not hurt anyone and are less likely to bounce into others' space.

3

Beanbag Blitz

Students experience working with beanbags to reinforce position words.

Essential Question

What are position words?

Curriculum Concepts

- Position words —
  over/under
  in/out
  off/on
  in front/behind
  near/far
  between

Physical Education National Standard(s)

Standard 2

Materials

- Beanbags (1 or 2 per student)

Steps to Success

Step 1

Ask students the essential question "What are position words?"

Step 2

Have students think about safety issues for being inside the classroom. Review classroom safety guidelines.

Step 3

Ask students to find personal space in the room.

Step 4

Give each student one or two beanbags (preferably two, one for each hand). Ask students to find different ways to toss the beanbags up in the air and catch them. Have students add the words TOSS and CATCH as they are exploring. Ask for someone to share the ways they were tossing and catching. Have the rest of the class watch and then try out the student's ideas. Have several other students share as the rest of the class copies.

Step 5

Use verbal directions to ask students to touch their beanbags to the following body parts: knees, wrist, chin, and feet. Then ask students to watch and copy as you put the beanbags on your body: head, stomach, shoulders, and back.

Step 6

Ask students to watch and copy as you put the beanbags in different places. First, put the beanbags *over* your head and ask the students where the beanbags are now. Then put the beanbags *under* your knees and ask the question *"Where are our beanbags now?"* Keep moving the beanbags to different places around your body to represent different position words. Have students identify where you place the beanbags, using position words.

Step 7

Use verbal directions to ask students to place the beanbags according to the position words you use. Look for students' comprehension to make sure they understand the position words. For example, you might say, "Put one beanbag *on* your knee and the other *over* your shoulder," then check to see that students' movements reflect an understanding of the positions you have mentioned.

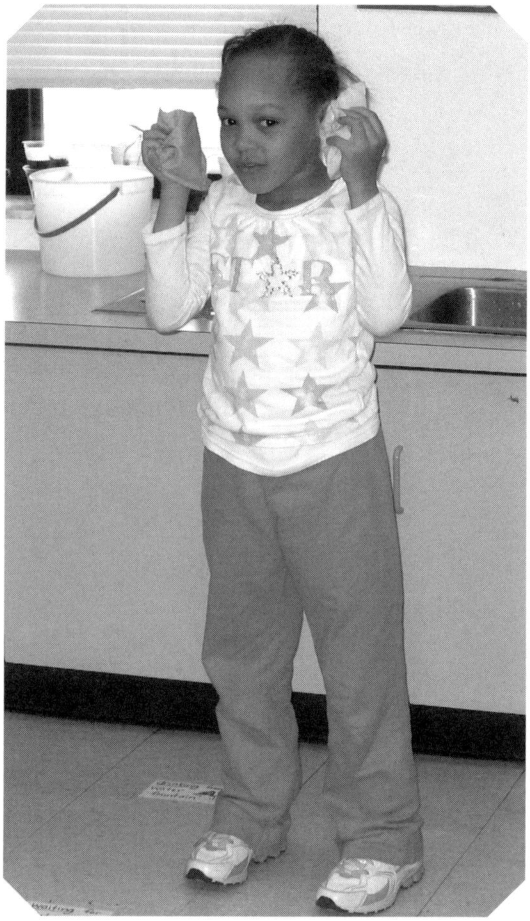

Position words are part of this student's learning as she follows the leader's verbal directions to put the beanbags near her ears.

Facilitation and Reflection

Ask students the following questions to help them reflect on their experiences and extend their thinking:

- *What did we learn about using our beanbags today?*
- *Name some position words.*

4

Exploring Pathways

Students use yarn to create straight, curved, and zigzag pathways.

Essential Question

What do you know about pathways?

Curriculum Concepts

- Straight, curved, and zigzag pathways
- Locomotor movement

Physical Education National Standard(s)

Standards 1, 2

Materials

- 7-foot-long piece of yarn for each student
- Cards with straight, zigzag, curved, and other shaped pathways drawn on them, as in the following examples:

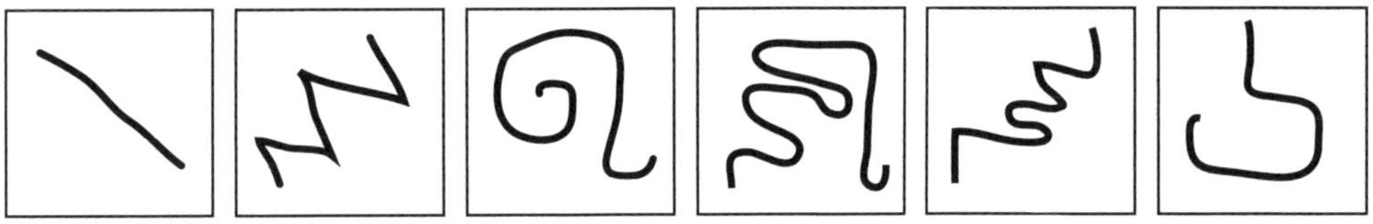

Steps to Success

Step 1

Ask students the essential question "What do you know about pathways?" Explain that pathways are either straight, curved, or zigzag. Pathways may also be a combination of two or more pathways put together. Pathways are used to get from one place to another.

Step 2

Ask students to try out moving their bodies as they explore the different pathways: straight, curved, and zigzag. For example, Jonathan skips in a straight pathway.

Step 3

Students explore making straight, curved, and zigzag pathways with yarn on the floor. After the students make a pathway with their yarn, have them choose a locomotor movement to do alongside each of the pathways. Have students take turns being the leader and sharing their pathway and their movement. Everyone copies the leader's movement.

Step 4

Students choose one or more pathway cards to copy with their yarn on the floor. They choose a different locomotor movement for each different pathway. Felix chose the card with the question mark on it, as seen in the photo below. He decided to jump for the straight part of the pathway, and he skipped for the curved part.

After the student creates the shape of the question mark with yarn on the floor, he will choose how to move along the pathway he created.

Step 5

Ask students to shape their piece of yarn into a letter of the alphabet. Ask them to notice what pathways are in their letter and choose a locomotor movement for each pathway in their letter. Ask the students to make the sound of the letter as they travel the pathways in their letter. For example, Paul made the letter "P" and said the letter had a straight pathway and a curved pathway. He decided to run for the straight pathway and he walked backward for the curved pathway. As Paul was moving to make the pathways, he was saying the sound of the letter *P.*

Step 6

Have students repeat Step 4 using their favorite number.

Step 7

Have students work with a partner to create the pathways for two-letter words or two-digit numbers. Examples of two-letter words might include *go, to, no, by, ah, at.* Have partners travel along the pathways using locomotor movements. Ask the partners to describe the pathways used in their words.

Facilitation and Reflection

Ask students the following questions to help them reflect on their experiences and extend their thinking:

- *How are straight, curved, and zigzag pathways the same or different?*
- *Which pathways were the easiest or most difficult to travel?*
- *When do you ever have to travel in pathways?* Students might offer answers such as, "I have to walk on the sidewalk to my classroom outside," or "It goes straight and then zigzag."
- *Where else do you notice pathways?* In giving responses, students may name objects in your classroom. They may also talk about the pathways that make up letters and numbers.

Extensions

For second grade:

Students get in groups of three. Each student in the group chooses a different pathway to make with his or her piece of yarn. Students connect their pieces of yarn to the yarn of the others in their group. The group chooses three different locomotor movements to represent each pathway and to use to travel alongside the yarn. After the students in each group of three has had a chance to travel their own connected pathways, they will visit other groups. The students will travel alongside the new connected pathways using locomotor movements they have chosen to represent each pathway. Repeat Step 7 using three-letter words, three-digit numbers, or geometric shapes.

5

Exploring Striking

Students explore the skill of striking using lightweight paddles and balls.

Essential Questions

What is striking? What are some factors that affect striking?

Curriculum Concepts

- Manipulative skill — striking
- Spatial awareness — space for striking

Physical Education National Standard(s)

Standard 1

Materials

- Lollipop paddles
- Yarn balls, foam balls, tennis balls, whiffle balls, rubber balls

Steps to Success

Step 1

Ask students the essential questions "What is striking? What are some factors that affect striking?" Ask students to explore all the different ways they can use their lollipop paddle and foam ball together. Remind students to stay in their own space and watch out for other students. Walk around and provide language and comments to students about the ways they are trying to strike the ball or use the paddle and ball together.

Step 2

Ask for volunteers to share with the class how they used their paddle and ball. For example, if John demonstrates how he hit his ball straight up in the air, have the class copy and try John's idea. Ask students how they moved their paddle to hit the ball. Sally might say, "I swung my paddle up." Have several more students show how they used their paddle and ball and have the class copy each. Ask questions to help students compare and contrast the different movements as new students perform their idea.

Note: This exploration and sharing time could take an entire class period. Keep in mind that, the younger the student, the more eager he or she is to share his or her idea.

Step 3

Ask students to put their foam balls away. Then tell them you are going to send them to one side of the court (play area) where they will find a different object (ball) to try and strike with their paddle. Count the number of students present and send half of the students to the other side. Students will take with them the paddle they were using in Step 2. Allow students to explore with the new ball and paddle for 4–5 minutes, and then have the students switch to the other side (station). Have students explore for another 4–5 minutes with the new ball at the other station. *Note:* Some students may try hitting with a partner.

This student develops spatial awareness as she practices striking a ball using a lollipop paddle.

Facilitation and Reflection

Ask students the following questions to help them reflect on their experiences and extend their thinking:

- *What did you discover you had to do to be successful at striking?*
- *How did the different sizes and kinds of balls affect striking?*

Extensions

Have students focus their striking so the object goes forward as the student uses a sideways swinging pattern. The arm action should be back-to-front.

6

Fitness Routine

Students make up a fitness routine using locomotor movements for the A section of a musical recording and nonlocomotor movements for the B section of the music.

Essential Question

What are some movements we can do to increase our heart rate?

Curriculum Concepts

- Locomotor movement
- Nonlocomotor movement
- Sequencing
- Basic timing

Physical Education National Standard(s)

Standards 1, 2, 3

Materials

- Recording of "Yankee Doodle" (on accompanying CD)

Using Recorded Music for Movement Activities

The A section is the first section of a recording or song after the introduction. For example, if singing "Yankee Doodle," the A section would be the first part of the song. The B section is the second part of the song. When using the recording, you will hear the change from the A section to the B section. When using recorded music, we suggest using locomotor movements for the A section and nonlocomotor movements for the B section. A *simplify* strategy for when you are beginning to use music as a fitness routine is to have students select one locomotor movement and one nonlocomotor movement, performing those movements through two repetitions of the music. As you and the students get comfortable, you can make up fitness routines, changing the locomotor and nonlocomotor movements on every section.

Steps to Success

Step 1

Ask students the essential question "What are some movements we can do to increase our heart rate?" After you discuss with the class some movements needed to increase their heart rate, explain that the class is going to create a fitness routine. This routine will use locomotor and nonlocomotor movements that the students feel will increase their heart rate. Ask students to explore a variety of locomotor movements in place. Some students may march with their knees high, some may march with their feet apart, and others may take steps with their feet pointing in or out. Some students may jump or hop. Encourage the students to take turns sharing their movements as the rest of the class copies and describes the movements.

What is Your Heart Rate?

Your **heart rate** is the rate at which your heart beats, usually measured in beats per minute. Heart rate is usually used to obtain a quick evaluation of a person's health.

How Do You Measure Your Heart Rate?

Your heart rate can be measured at any spot on your body at which an artery is close to the surface and a pulse can be felt. The most common places to measure heart rate using the palpation method is at the wrist (radial artery) and the neck (carotid artery). You should always use your fingers to take a pulse, not your thumb, particularly when recording someone else's pulse, as you can sometimes feel your own pulse through your thumb.

Manual Method

- Carotid Pulse (neck) — To take your heart rate at the neck, place your first two fingers on either side of the neck. Being careful not to press too hard, count the number of beats for one minute.
- Radial Pulse (wrist) — Place your index and middle fingers together on the opposite wrist, about one-half inch on the inside of the joint, in line with the index finger. Once you find a pulse, count the number of beats you feel within a one-minute period.

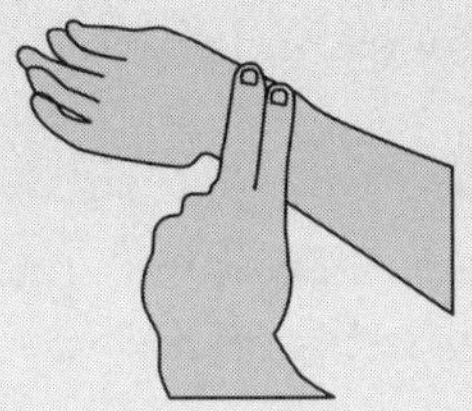

Step 2

Use the recording of "Yankee Doodle" (found on the CD in the back of this book) and have students do a locomotor movement as you play the A section, or the first section of the music. Ask students for examples of locomotor movements that can be done to the music. The students decide what locomotor movement they want to do for the first A section of the fitness routine. Write the students' examples on chart paper or the whiteboard (see "Example of a Fitness Routine to Music" on p. 56). Be sure to make this as interactive as possible. The students should be coming up with the labels for the movements for the A section.

Step 3

Ask the students to explore nonlocomotor movements they can do with their hands or arms. For example, a student might choose to swing both arms back and forth. Have students explore different movements. Ask the students to take turns sharing their movement(s) as the class copies. Have the class decide what nonlocomotor movement they want to use for the fitness routine that goes with the B section of the music.

Step 4

Play the recording again and have students do a locomotor movement to section A of the music and then a nonlocomotor movement to section B. Have the students go back to the chart and write down movements (or you can write them) for section B of the music as they did in Step 2.

Step 5

Practice doing the routine using learner SAY & DO before putting the music back on.

Example of a Fitness Routine to Music

Fitness Routine to Music

Introduction: 8 beats; **Musical Form:** AB (6 times) — "Yankee Doodle"
Notice how the fitness routine allows for repetition. This is especially important with students in kindergarten and first grade.

Facilitation and Reflection

Locomotor Movements			Nonlocomotor Movements	
1.	A	Marching (knees high)	B	Patting knees
2.	A	Marching (knees high)	B	Patting knees
3.	A	Jumping	B	Shaking both hands
4.	A	Jumping	B	Shaking both hands
5.	A	Walking forward (general space)	B	Swinging both arms
6.	A	Walking forward (general space)	B	Swinging both arms

Ask students the following questions to help them reflect on their experiences and extend their thinking:

- *What was your favorite locomotor movement?*
- *What was your favorite nonlocomotor movement?*
- *How did you know when to change your movements?*
- *What were some of the movements that made you work the hardest and increase your heart rate?*

Extensions

For second grade:

After students have entered the second grade, you can begin to do dances that have specific steps. We suggest not doing formal dances with students until second grade or older. Below is a dance to the recording "Yankee Doodle" that you can try with your students after they have had many experiences with fitness routines to music. This dance is done in a circle with no hands held. Be sure to wait for the 8-beat introduction before starting movement.

Yankee Doodle*

(United States)

Part I

FWD	FWD	FWD	FWD	BWD	BWD	BWD	BWD

IN	IN	IN	IN	OUT	OUT	OUT	OUT

Beats

1–4 Four steps forward counterclockwise
5–8 Four steps backward clockwise
9–12 Four steps toward center of circle
13–16 Four steps away from center

Note: No R foot or L foot needs to be specified.

Part II

HEEL	TOG	DOWN	UP	HEEL	TOG	DOWN	UP

KNEES		SHOULDERS		MARCH	MARCH	MARCH	MARCH

Beat

1 Extend one foot toward center, touching heel to floor
2 Step down on the same foot, bringing feet together
3 Bend knees
4 Straighten knees
5–8 Repeat beats 1–4 with opposite footwork
9–10 Touch knees with both hands
11–12 Touch shoulders with both hands
13–16 March in place four steps

Note: No R foot or L foot needs to be specified.

**Choreographed by Phyllis S. Weikart.*

7

Force: Light or Strong?

Students explore moving their bodies while using light and strong force.

Essential Question

What is force?

Curriculum Concepts

- Body awareness
- Force — light and strong
- Locomotor movement
- Nonlocomotor movement

Physical Education National Standard(s)

Standards 1, 2

Materials

- None

Steps to Success

Step 1

Ask students the essential question "What do you know about force?" Then ask students what has to happen for their bodies to move with force.

Step 2

Have students explore different ways to move their bodies while using force. For example, a student may stand still and use her arms to make a movement to show how strong she is. Another student might move around the room like a butterfly, showing light force. Still another student might use strong force by stomping around the room. Ask for volunteers to share their movements that use force, and have the other students copy the leader. Ask students to describe the amount of force they used to perform the movement. Together, have the class label the movement as using strong or light force. Then ask another student to share a movement using force (try to choose someone who was using the opposite force in his or her movement). Have the rest of the class copy the movement. Compare and contrast movements to reinforce the difference between light and strong force.

Step 3

Have students think about times when they might need to use light force. Try those movements with the whole class. An example of light force might be when you are trying to be quiet and sneak in without being seen so your movements are soft, with your feet touching lightly on the floor. Ask students what their light-force movement might sound like, and have students add sound to their favorite light-force movement. For example, a student flying like a bird using very soft movements might whisper or softly say *oooooo*.

Step 4

Repeat the process of Step 3 using the idea of strong force, such as when you are trying to kick a ball really hard.

Step 5

Have the students find a partner. Ask each student to choose his or her favorite movement-sound combination using light force. Have each partner share while the other partner copies.

Step 6

Repeat process of Step 5 using strong force.

Facilitation and Reflection

Ask students the following questions to help them reflect on their experiences and extend their thinking:

- *What did adding sounds to your movement do?*
- *Why is it important to use different amounts of force?*

Extensions

Use tennis balls for further exploration of contrast between light and strong force. Use balls that bounce in such a way to allow students to talk about light and strong force.

8

The Galloping Game

The focus for this activity is transitioning from galloping to skipping. Some students have a hard time being able to skip. This activity allows students to begin to "feel the skip" in their body.

Essential Questions

What is locomotor movement? What are the names of some of the locomotor movements we do in class?

Curriculum Concepts

- Locomotor movements (galloping, skipping)

Physical Education National Standard(s)

Standard 1

Materials

- Hand drum

Steps to Success

Step 1

Ask students the essential questions "What is locomotor movement? What are the names of some of the locomotor movements we do in class?" Ask students to warm up by doing different locomotor movements. Have students take turns being the leader and sharing their favorite locomotor movement (for example, marching, galloping, sliding, running, crawling, jumping, hopping); all students copy the leader's movement. Make sure students get practice galloping, hopping, and sliding. Have them practice alternating which foot is the lead foot during each of these movements.

Step 2

Model galloping for students, first using your right foot as the lead foot and then, without stopping, changing your lead foot to your left foot. Ask students what they noticed when you did this.

Step 3

Have students explore galloping and switching the foot that is the lead foot on their own.

Step 4

Ask students to watch as you model learner SAY & DO by galloping eight times and saying the word GALLOP each time. After the eighth time, say CHANGE and change your lead foot. With the new foot as the leader, do learner SAY & DO by galloping and saying the word GALLOP for each movement. Have students try this.

Step 5

Tell the students that now everyone is going to play The Galloping Game. Have students start out by galloping with their favorite foot as the lead foot. Each time they hear a drum, whistle, or the word CHANGE, they switch the lead foot. Start the game with long intervals between the signals. As students get comfortable with the idea and movements, shorten the time between signals. The goal is to get to where you are saying CHANGE or signaling every time the lead foot should change. After a few tries, stop the students. Ask students what happened to their gallop as the intervals between signals become shorter (Some students will notice they began to skip instead of gallop).

Step 6

Ask students to do eight gallops, then switch feet, then do eight more gallops. Then have students decrease the number of gallops between the changes. (For example, have students gallop 6, then 4, and then 2 times.) To demonstrate a gallop, you can show students that first they have one foot in front as the lead foot. Then weight is transferred from the back foot to the front foot several times using uneven timing. Then students stop and put the other foot in front and repeat the above sequence.

Step 7

Review skipping and talk about how The Galloping Game helps students to skip.

Facilitation and Reflection

Ask students the following questions to help them reflect on their experiences and extend their thinking:

- *Describe the locomotor movement of galloping.*
- *What two locomotor skills combine to make skipping?*

This student experiences the weight transfer that is part of skipping.

9

Jumping and Landing

Students will explore jumping off a low step, landing on a mat. Students will discuss the different type of jumps they tried and they will identify parts of a jump (takeoff, flight time, and landing). Buoyant and yielding landings will also be discussed.

Essential Question

What do you know about jumping?

Curriculum Concepts

- Jumping
- Landing – yielding and buoyant landing
- Yielding landing
- Buoyant landing

Physical Education National Standard(s)

Standards 1, 2

Materials

- Stack of two fitness (aerobic) steps or a platform (no more than 12 inches high)
- One mat for each platform

Steps to Success

Step 1

Ask students the essential question, "What do you know about jumping?" Students will share in their own words what they know about jumping. Some of their responses may include comments like the following: "Take off on both feet," "You have to bend your knees," or "Lift off the ground."

Step 2

Have the students explore different ways of jumping off the steps and landing on the mats, trying to stay balanced and landing on both feet. Ask students to share their favorite jump. Students will take turns being the leader and showing their jump to the class as everyone tries to copy the leader's jump. After all students have tried the leader's jump, ask the students to describe how they were jumping off the steps. Use students' examples of jumping to identify the three parts of a jump — takeoff, flight time, and landing.

Step 3

Ask students to think about their favorite jump. Have students try the jump again while thinking about the different parts of the jump. Students should be thinking about the takeoff, flight time, and landing. Ask students to say the parts of the favorite jump out loud as they are performing the jump. Circulate around the classroom, observing the different jumps and asking facilitating questions. These questions should draw students' attention to what they are doing during their jump.

Step 4

Have the students explore different ways of taking off. Also have them explore doing something during their flight time before landing on both feet. For example, a student can jump from the step using both feet, and while in his flight time, the student can bend both legs and straighten out both arms. Then have students take turns being the leader and showing the entire class what they did. Ask all the students to copy the leader and describe the movements they did during takeoff and during their flight time while copying.

Step 5

Introduce the terms *buoyant* and *yielding* as they pertain to landings (see the sidebar below). Have the students explore both of these landings.

Step 6

Ask students to make a three-part plan that includes the following:

1. A way to take off
2. A movement to do during flight time
3. An ending that includes either a buoyant or a yielding landing

Different Kinds of Landings

Buoyant landing — When you spring up quickly after each jump.

Yielding landing — When you bend your knees to absorb the force when you land, as if sinking into the floor.

Step 7

Have students share their plan and talk about the three parts of their plan with a partner, the class, or the teacher.

Facilitation and Reflection

Ask students the following questions to help them reflect on their experiences and extend their thinking:

- *What helped you to go high or far with your jump?*
- *Which landing did you choose, and why?*
- *When do you ever have to use a buoyant or a yielding landing?* Students might say that they use a buoyant landing when jumping rope and that they use a yielding landing when jumping down from the monkey bars.

10

Jump, Jump, Jump

Students experience different ways to jump.

Essential Question

What is jumping?

Curriculum Concepts

- Locomotor movement (skill) — jump

Physical Education National Standard(s)

Standard 1

Materials

- Hula hoops, one for each student (used in activity extensions, below)

Steps to Success

Step 1

Ask students the essential question "What is jumping?" Have the students watch and copy as you jump in the air, bending your knees, swinging your arms up in the air, and landing on both feet at the same time. (Do several jumps, pausing between jumps). Have students join you when they feel comfortable.

Step 2

Ask students to describe how their bodies were moving when they were jumping. Ask them what they did to make their body go up in the air. Be sure to point out that *a jump* is when both feet land on the ground at the same time.

Step 3

Have the students explore all the different ways they can jump. Walk around the room and comment, copy, and provide language that describes how individual students are jumping. For example, perhaps you copy Rachel's jump. After you and Rachel do several of Rachel's jumps together, you might say, "Rachel, you started your jump on one foot and then you jumped in the air and landed on two feet."

Note: With young students it is very important to provide language in complete sentences.

Step 4

Have students share their jumps by taking turns being the leader. Once the leader shows his or her jump, have the whole class try it out. Ask the students questions that help them think about how the jumps are similar and how they are different. For example, you might say, "Kristy, how was your jump different from Jorge's jump?"

Note: If working with kindergarteners, this step may take the entire class period. These students like to share, and it is important to ask questions and allow all students to show their jump.

Many times during this step a student will do a movement and call it jump when it is really a hop. It is important to take that opportunity to discuss, and have students experience, the difference between a jump and a hop. Remember that the landing determines whether it is a jump or a hop. **If the landing is on two feet then it is a jump, and if the landing is on one foot, it is a hop.**

A jump always has a two-foot landing, which this student demonstrates.

Facilitation and Reflection

Ask students the following questions to help them reflect on their experiences and extend their thinking:

- *What do we call a jump?*
- *How does your weight transfer when jumping?*
- *What roles do bending your knees and swinging your arms play in performing a jump?*

Extensions

Provide each student with a hula hoop and allow students time to explore playing with the hula hoop. Ask students to find different ways they can jump using the hula hoop. Have students take turns sharing while the entire class copies. Students may choose to jump using the hula hoop like a jump rope, or they may choose to put the hula hoop on the ground and jump over, in, out, and so forth.

11

Levels

Students make statues to experience the difference between high, middle, and low levels.

Essential Question

How can we move our bodies at different levels?

Curriculum Concepts

- Space awareness — levels (high, middle, low)
- Locomotor movement
- Nonlocomotor movement

Physical Education National Standard(s)

Standards 1, 2, 5

Materials

- Recordings of "Yankee Doodle" and "Joe Clark Mixer" (on accompanying CD)

Steps to Success

Step 1

Ask students the essential question, "How can we move our bodies at different levels?" Show students examples of levels using your body. Have students try making statues (making a pose and freezing there) with their bodies at different levels. For example, one student may put his hands and knees on the floor to show a low level. Another student may stand up tall with her hands in the air to demonstrate a high level. Students take turns being the leader and sharing their statue. Other students copy the movement and name the level it incorporates.

Step 2

Ask the students how the body can represent the different levels (high, middle, and low). Discuss with the students how levels can be demonstrated on their bodies. For example, *high* can be represented on the body from the chest and up; *middle* can be represented between the knees and chest; and *low* could be represented below the knees. Point to these different areas of your body as you explain levels to students.

Step 3

Have students choose a partner. One student in each pair will make a statue at one of the three levels (high, middle, or low). The partner copies the statue and tells the leader the level of the statue. Have each pair switch leaders. As the students work on this step, encourage them to use language to describe their statues. For example, Marcus and Tommy are partners. Marcus is the leader first and stands on his tiptoes and puts his arms in the air. Tommy copies the movement and tells Marcus the statue is high and that he had to stretch his arms above his head while standing on his tiptoes.

These two students make statues with their bodies at a medium level.

Step 4

Up to this point, students have been working with levels to create statues, or frozen movements. Have students apply their knowledge of levels to nonlocomotor movement. Encourage students to use different body parts to explore the high, middle, and low levels. Encourage students to share their movements with the class as the other students copy the leader.

Step 5

Have students explore using levels with locomotor movement. Use the same procedure as described in Step 4.

Facilitation and Reflection

Ask students the following questions to help them reflect on their experiences and extend their thinking:

- *Which level(s) were the hardest? Which were the easiest?*
- *When might you put your body at different levels?*
- *What did you discover about levels when you were using nonlocomotor and locomotor movements?*

Extensions

Use a few sections of instrumental recorded music such as "Yankee Doodle" or "Joe Clark Mixer" and have students use locomotor movements to represent different levels. Encourage students to move at that level for one phrase of music before changing to another level. Both "Yankee Doodle" and "Joe Clark Mixer" have 16 walking beats.

12

Locomotor Movement

Students explore locomotor movements and discuss how one transfers weight when performing the different movements.

Essential Question

What is a locomotor movement?

Curriculum Concepts

- Locomotor movement
- Weight transfer

Physical Education National Standard(s)

Standard 1

Materials

- None

Steps to Success

Step 1

Ask students the essential question "What is a locomotor movement?" Explain to students that a locomotor movement is a movement that does not involve keeping a body part anchored to the floor. When you do a locomotor movement you have to transfer weight from one body part to another. Locomotor movements can be done in personal space or general space. Have students explore different ways they can move and travel with their bodies. As the students are moving, ask them to think about *how* their bodies move. For example, you might say, "What are you having to do with your legs when you are galloping?"

Step 2

Walk around the room to individually comment on and copy students' movements. Provide language labeling the movement a student is doing. For example, you might say, "John, I see you are using the locomotor movement jumping. You are landing on both feet."

Step 3

Ask for volunteers to share their favorite locomotor movement with the class. For example, when Tabitha was the leader, she galloped across the room and the class copied Tabitha's movement. The teacher asked the class what to call the movement that Tabitha shared. Be sure to encourage other students to be the leader and share their locomotor movements as the rest of the class tries them out. Ask open-ended questions (see p. 13) to help facilitate students' understanding of what their bodies have to do to perform the locomotor movement. (For example, you might say, "What did your body have to do when you were crawling on the floor?") Also ask students to compare and contrast the movements shared. For example, you might ask how John's locomotor movement was different from Tabitha's. The students might answer, "We were jumping," "We landed on both feet," "Tabitha was galloping," or "We were on one foot and then the other."

What Do We Mean By *Facilitate?*

Facilitate is a component of the *Education Through Movement (ETM)* teaching model, in which the teacher uses varied strategies involving action, thought, and language to engage learners and enable them to construct their own knowledge. It is important to use open-ended questions. When asking students questions, be sure to begin with words like *why, how, compare, contrast, tell me about* and *where.*

Step 4

Ask students if they know what is happening to their body weight as they are doing the locomotor movements. Have the students try their movement again and pay attention to where their weight is when they are doing each part of the movement.

Step 5

Ask the students to watch and copy. Begin by taking deliberate steps, moving in general space, as students copy. Ask students to pay attention to how their body feels as their body weight transfers from one foot to the other. Explain that this is how we know we are doing a locomotor movement — our weight transfers from one foot to the other. Explain that walking is an *alternating* weight transfer and that it is one example of a locomotor movement.

Step 6

Ask students to try all the locomotor movements the class has done together for this activity. Have the students think about how their weight is transferring as they practice the movements. The students should mention the weight transfer of the hop, jump, gallop, and skip.

Facilitation and Reflection

Ask students the following questions to help them reflect on their experiences and extend their thinking:

- *What makes a movement locomotor?*
- *What are the names of the locomotor skills we tried today?*
- *What are the different ways to transfer weight as we move around the room?*

13

Long Jump Rope (Pre-Jump Rope Skill Progression)

Children explore jumping without and then with a jump rope to develop balance, strength, coordination, and timing.

Essential Questions

What is a jump?

What do you have to do differently to jump a long rope rather than an individual (shorter) rope?

Curriculum Concepts

- Locomotor skill — jump
- Timing
- Balance

Physical Education National Standard(s)

Standard 1

Materials

- Long jump ropes (approx. 10 feet) — enough for each pair of students

Steps to Success

Step 1

Ask students the essential questions "What is a jump? What do you have to do differently to jump a long rope rather than an individual (shorter) rope?" Place a long jump rope flat and straight on the ground or floor. Have students work at each rope in pairs. Ask students to explore jumping over the rope as it lies on the ground or floor. Ask for student volunteers, one at a time, to share how they were jumping, and have the class copy each student's jump. Ask for other volunteers to share their jump and have the class copy. Ask questions that encourage students to compare and contrast the way students were jumping over the rope.

Step 2

Ask students to try their jumps again, this time using learner SAY & DO. Have them add the word JUMP each time they land on the floor. This will help the students jump in a steady way, which begins to build timing.

Proceed to the following steps as students are ready:

Step 3

If possible, anchor one end of the jump ropes to a wall or fence. Have a student stand at the end of the rope that is not anchored. If you are unable to anchor one end of the rope, have a student at each end of the rope. Ask students to watch and copy your arm swinging from side to side in front of your body without the rope. Have students try it out (without the rope). Then have students try the same movement with the other arm.

Step 4

Ask students to do the same movement as in Step 3, but this time have students use the rope. The rope swings back and forth with the side-to-side arm movement. Be sure the rope is not turning all the way around. Be sure students try the movement using the other arm.

Step 5

Have students watch as you begin swinging the rope from side to side. Ask students to listen to the words you say with each movement. Say the word READY to set up for the swing (your arm is in front of your body at this point, ready to swing or turn); as you swing your arm out to the side, say the word SWING, and say the word JUMP each time the rope hits the ground. The rope is swinging side to side at this point but not going over in an arc.

Have the students try swinging the rope side to side by adding the words READY, SWING, JUMP. Be sure that each pair is moving the rope in their own timing rather than whole-class timing.

Ask students what they notice about the rope swinging when they added the words READY, SWING, JUMP. Some may say, "The rope slowed down," or "The rope moved in steady beat." You might say, "When we swing the rope in a steady beat, someone can jump in the middle."

Step 6

Ask a student to stand next to the midsection of the stationary rope. Have the student swinging the rope as well as the jumper use learner SAY & DO to begin swinging the rope: they say READY, SWING, JUMP. The student jumping jumps over the rope as it is swinging back and forth. Then everyone uses learner SAY & DO. After a couple of minutes, switch jumpers and swingers. Get new swingers started with learner SAY & DO: READY, SWING, JUMP. Jumpers jump.

Step 7

Demonstrate how to turn the rope all the way around by turning your arm in a circle in front of your

The student is turning his arm in a circle in front of him to turn the rope.

body. Have students try this movement and then try it using the other arm. Students should use the learner SAY & DO words READY, SWING, JUMP with the movements. Walk around to the groups, checking the speed of the rope (making sure the rope is not turning too slowly or too quickly for the student jumping the rope) and making sure the swingers are making a circle with their arm.

Step 8

Add a jumper to each rope. Ask one student to stand next to the midsection of the rope. Say READY, SWING, JUMP and have the student try jumping the turning rope when you say JUMP.

Facilitation and Reflection

Ask students the following questions to help them reflect on their experiences and extend their thinking:

- As the jumper: *What do you know about trying to jump the rope?*
- As the turner: *What must you do so the jumper can successfully jump the rope?*

14

Lummi Stick Fun

Students use Lummi sticks to make different sequences and to create patterns.

Essential Questions

What do you know about patterns? What do you know about sequences?

Curriculum Concepts

- Patterns/sequences
- Spatial awareness
- Timing

Physical Education National Standard(s)

Standards 1, 2

Materials

- Lummi sticks (2 sticks per student; Lummi sticks are hardwood cylindrical sticks, usually about 7 inches long and .75 in diameter, and they are used as a percussive musical instrument; they can be purchased from teacher supply stores and physical education and music catalogs)

Steps to Success

Step 1

Ask students the essential questions "What do you know about patterns? What do you know about sequences?" and have the whole class participate in discussing the questions.

Step 2

Remind the students to think about safety issues that relate to being inside the classroom while using objects. Have students review the basic safety reminders.

Step 3

Ask students to find a safe (personal) space in the classroom. Have each student take two Lummi sticks and in their personal space begin to explore the different ways they can use the sticks. After a few minutes, ask for several volunteers to share what they did with the sticks. For example, one student might say she was scraping one stick on the other; another student might say he was hitting the two sticks together at each end. Have the entire class try what the leader demonstrates. Ask the class questions about the movements the students are sharing. For example, you might ask how students' movements with the sticks are similar or different. In the case of a leader who incorporates tapping, you might ask how many times the leader tapped the floor.

Step 4

Ask students to "watch and copy" as you hit the floor two times with the sticks and then hit the sticks together two times. (See page 10 for a discussion of watch and copy.) Have the students join you doing the movements continuously when the students get the pattern. Everyone repeats the pattern several times. Using the strategy of learner SAY & DO, begin to add words to the pattern, such as FLOOR, FLOOR, TAP, TAP. Ask students to describe the pattern they created. During this discussion, talk to students about timing. For example, you might say, "Did you notice that when we put words to our actions and said the words together, we were able to stay in the same timing?"

Step 5

Ask students to come up with 4-beat patterns of their own. Encourage the students to make up several patterns. After a few minutes, ask them to choose their favorite pattern and label their movements with words. Then ask students to take turns being the leader and sharing their 4-beat pattern. For example, one student might share her four-beat pattern with the words FLOOR, HEAD, KNEES, and FLOOR. Everyone copies, doing the movements as they say the words.

Step 6

Ask the students to find a partner. Together, the partners put their own favorite pattern together. Remind the students to do their pattern and then add the words to their pattern — that is, to use learner SAY & DO. Partners share their 8-beat patterns with the rest of the class as the class copies.

Facilitation and Reflection

Ask students the following questions to help them reflect on their experiences and extend their thinking:

- *How did putting words to your movements help?*
- *What is timing?*

Extensions

For older students:
Have two sets of partners get together to make a group of four; have them try to create a 16-beat pattern.

15

Making Body Shapes

Students explore making four body shapes (wide, narrow, round and twisted) and matching the body shapes of a partner.

Essential Question

What are some words we use to describe shapes that we can make with our bodies?

Curriculum Concepts

- Relationships between one's body parts

Physical Education National Standard(s)

Standards 1, 2, 5

Materials

- Cards with stick-figure poses — see examples at the end of this activity.

Steps to Success

Step 1

Ask students the essential question "What are some words we use to describe shapes we can make with our bodies?" Discuss the meaning of the vocabulary words *wide, narrow, round,* and *twisted*. The teacher models how students can make the shapes with their bodies.

Step 2

Have students explore making the four shapes with their bodies (wide, narrow, round, and twisted). Students will take turns being the leader and sharing their shape with the class. Everyone copies the leader and describes the shapes.

This student demonstrates how to make a twisted shape with her body.

Step 3

Show the students various stick-figure cards. Students use their bodies to match the shape represented on the stick-figure cards, and they label each pose as wide, narrow, round, or twisted.

Step 4

Have students work in pairs. One student makes a statue in one of the four body shapes and the partner copies and labels the shape. The students continue until each partner has taken several turns and has had the opportunity to make all four body shapes in various ways.

After the teacher holds up a stick figure shape on a card, the students copy the shape with their own bodies.

Facilitation and Reflection

Ask students the following questions to help them reflect on their experiences and extend their thinking:

- *What did you find out about the body shapes of wide, narrow, round, and twisted?* Students might give responses such as, "They are different," "When I'm wide my body is spread out," or "When I am round I look like a ball."
- *When do our bodies ever have to make these shapes?* Students may offer responses like the following: "When I bat I have to twist my body," "When I do a split at gymnastics I am wide," or "When I hang on the monkey bars I am narrow."
- *Where else have you seen these shapes?* Students may say something like "A pencil is narrow," "Balls are round," or "Pretzels are twisted."

16

Moving in Different Directions

Students explore traveling forward, backward, and sideward. Students choose a locomotor movement and move in a certain direction when hearing or seeing a visual cue.

Essential Question

What directions can your body travel?

Curriculum Concepts

- Spatial awareness — direction (forward, backward, sideward)
- Following directions
- Listening skills
- Locomotor movement

Physical Education National Standard(s)

Standards 1, 2

Materials

- 1 Hand drum

Steps to Success

Step 1

Ask students the essential question "What directions can your body travel?" Clarify what part of our body is leading when we travel in different directions. For example, if someone is moving sideward, their side or one leg is leading; if they are moving backward, their back is leading.

Step 2

Students explore locomotor movements in forward, backward, and sideward directions. Students take turns sharing their movement(s) with the class; the class copies the leader's movement.

Step 3

Use a hand drum and beat the drum once to represent forward, beat twice to represent backward, and beat three times to represent sideward. The students choose a locomotor movement and travel when the drum sounds. Students take turns using the drum and making up a new code for the direction and beats of the drum.

Gaining awareness of general space, students practice locomotor movement in different directions.

Step 4

Use visual signals to have students travel forward, backward, and sideward. Let students be leaders using the visual signals. A student might stand in front of the class and point to the direction in which he wants the other students to move. For example, if he points to the side, the students will move in a sideward direction.

Facilitation and Reflection

Ask students the following questions to help them reflect on their experiences and extend their thinking:

- *In which directions was it easiest or most difficult to travel and why?*
- *When do you ever have to travel in different directions?* Examples of children's responses include "We walk forward in a line," "I spin 'round and 'round," or "I have to go backward to catch a ball high in the air."

17

My Personal Space

Students explore personal space (the space around the body extending as far as the body and body parts can reach without touching other people or objects) while using locomotor and nonlocomotor movements. Students will use poly spots (flat polyvinyl circles) or carpet squares to define their space.

Essential Question

What is personal space?

Curriculum Concepts

- Personal space
- Locomotor movement
- Nonlocomotor movement
- Relationships with objects and/or people
- Position words
- Steady beat (used in the "Extensions" section of this activity)

Physical Education National Standard(s)

Standards 1, 2

Materials

- Carpet squares or poly spots (flat polyvinyl circles) for each student
- "Peat Fire Flame" (recording on accompanying CD)

Steps to Success

Step 1

Ask students the essential question "What is personal space?" Spread out carpet squares or poly spots around the room.

Step 2

Have students choose a spot (carpet square or poly spot). Ask students what they know about personal space.

Step 3

Ask students to explore movements they can do on the carpet square. After students have had time to explore, ask for volunteers to share their movement. When a student shares a movement, everyone else joins in and copies the movement. Ask questions about the movement after the students have had a chance to copy. For example, you might ask, "What was Minerva doing on her shape? How were we moving on our shape?"

Step 4

Ask students to explore ways they can move around the carpet square. Have students share their ideas with the entire class as the class copies the leader.

Step 5

Ask the students to compare and contrast the movements they did in Steps 3 and 4. Have students describe the different kinds of movements they were able to do in their personal space.

This student finds the right amount of personal space he needs to be able to perform movements without bumping into others.

Facilitation and Reflection

Ask students the following questions to help them reflect on their experiences and extend their thinking:

- *What types of movements did you do on the carpet square?*
- *What type of movements did you do around the carpet square?*
- *What do we need to remember when we are working in our personal space?* Examples of answers students might offer include "To keep enough space between myself and someone else" or "Start out with enough room so I can do what I want and not bother someone else."

Extensions

- Put on a musical selection such as "Peat Fire Flame" (on accompanying CD). Have students choose a movement they want to do **on** their carpet square. Play the music as the students do their movement to music.
- Have students plan a movement to do **around** the carpet square. Put on the same music.
- Have students explore movements that can be done **over** the carpet squares.

18

Pathway Maps

Students review straight, curved, and zigzag pathways by using their bodies in personal space. Students work alone or in pairs to create a pathway map using paper and pencil. After creating the pathway map, the students explore different locomotor movements to travel on the pathway map.

Essential Question

What do you know about pathways?

Curriculum Concepts

- Pathways — straight, curved, zigzag
- Locomotor movement
- Personal space
- General space

Physical Education National Standard(s)

Standards 1, 2, 5

Materials

- Paper
- Pencil
- 4 different objects placed apart from each other in the space (example — 4 cones that have different colors or different shapes, such as a rectangle, diamond, star, and triangle)

Steps to Success

Step 1

Ask students the essential question, "What do you know about pathways?" Explain that pathways can be curved, straight, or zigzag. Pathways can also be a combination of two or more pathways. Have students explore traveling in curved, zigzag, and straight pathways while using general space. Be sure students try out different locomotor movements when traveling the three pathways (curved, straight, and zigzag). Encourage students to share the locomotor movements they used with the pathways. Students take turns being the leader as everyone copies the leader's movements while traveling the different pathways. For example, Kristen was the leader, and she marched as she moved in a curved pathway.

Step 2

Students may choose to work in pairs or alone to create a pathway map with paper and pencil. Students must choose a starting marker (such as the blue cone) and label it on the pathway map as the starting point. Then they create a map traveling to each marker only once. The map must include the three pathways and must be labeled with three different ways to travel.

Students get "hands-on" experience with pathways by following the pathways map they created.

Step 3

After students create their map, they travel the map using the locomotor movements they have chosen to use.

Step 4

Students trade pathway maps with other students and try out a new pathway map. Example of a pathway map:

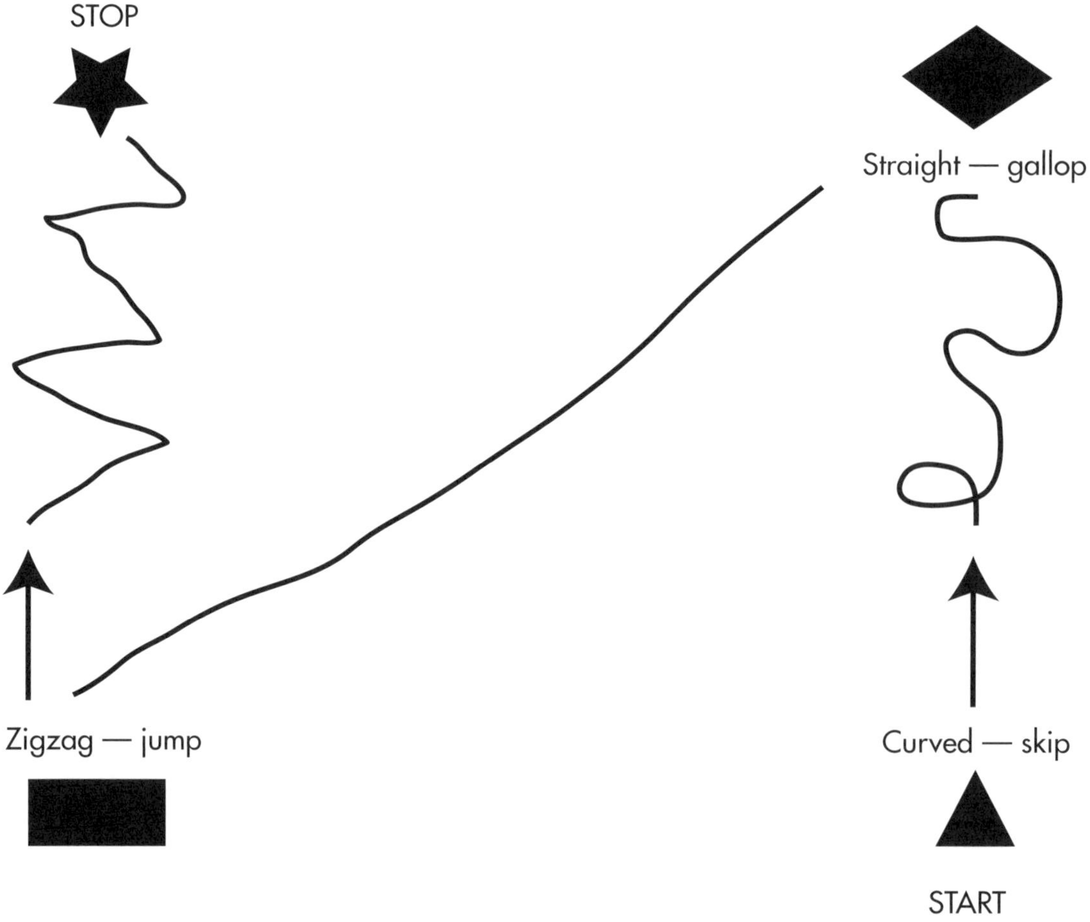

Here is an additional example of a pathway map, created by a student:

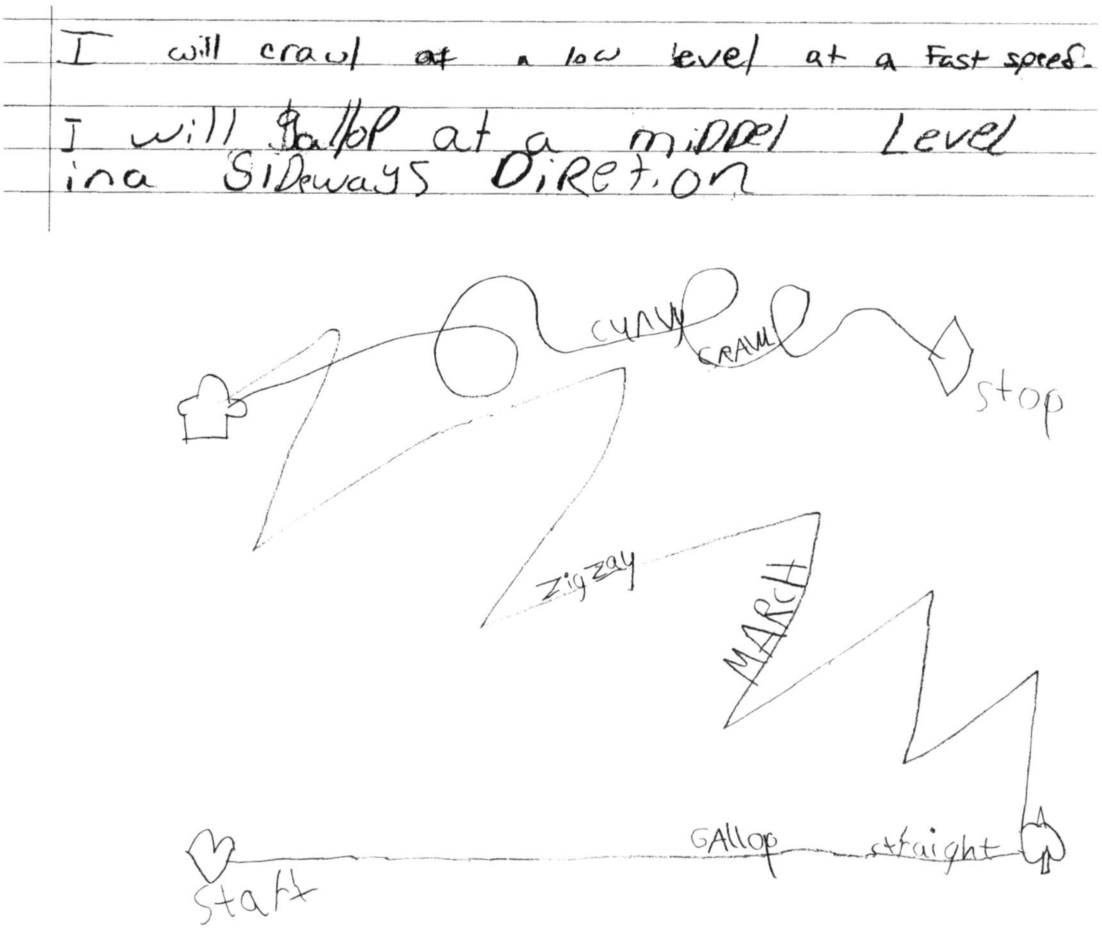

Facilitation and Reflection

Ask students the following questions to help them reflect on their experiences and extend their thinking:

- *Which locomotor movements were the most difficult to travel in pathways?*
- *What did you find out about following your own map, and what did you find out about following other students' maps?*
- *Name other times you have to travel in pathways.* For example, a student might say, "When I run on the jogging track" or "When I am at Disney World." You might say to students, "When we are on vacation we are traveling on the road, and it is a pathway."

Extensions

Have students do this activity at another time and add other concepts, such as direction and level, to the pathway maps.

19

Ready, Set, Turn

Students experience the progressions (the steps) of jumping a single rope.

Essential Questions

What is the most important step when jumping rope? Why do you think so?

Curriculum Concepts

- Locomotor movement — jump
- Timing

Physical Education National Standard(s)

Standard 1

Materials

- Jump rope for each student

Steps to Success

Step 1

Ask students the essential questions "What is the most important part of jumping rope? Why?" and have a class discussion about this.

Show students how to measure a jump rope to make sure they are using the correct size of rope for them. Have many different lengths of jump rope out for students to find and measure, making sure each student gets the right-sized rope. Ask students to find a personal space when they have the rope they are going to use and have the students explore jumping with the rope in their personal space.

Step 2

Ask students what they discovered when trying to turn the rope and jump at the same time. Students might say, "It was hard," or "I couldn't do it." Discuss with students that jumping rope is hard because it involves doing two things at the same time.

Step 3

Have the students put the ropes on the ground — students will not use them in this step. Ask students to watch and copy. First, show the "ready to jump position" (your hands are in front of your body at waist level); have students copy. Move your hands and arms down slowly toward the ground and then turn your arms back behind you and then raise them over your head, and finally draw them down in front of your body, making a complete circle; have the students copy. Have students practice this movement several times. Ask the students to think of words that will help them remember how to do the movement (use learner SAY & DO). For example, a student might use learner SAY & DO by using the words READY, DOWN, AROUND to represent the movement of turning the rope. Have the students try doing the movement and saying their words as they do the movement. Observe to make sure the first arm movement is down or the rope will not go over the students' head.

This student practices jumping the rope using learner SAY & DO.

Step 4

Ask students to pick up their ropes. Have students try to turn the rope while using the words they created in Step 3. Mention to students that they start with the rope behind their ankles. You might also suggest that students use their toes to catch the rope. Remind the students to keep their eyes straight ahead, watching for the rope to swing over their head. Have students work on turning the rope and then stopping between each sequence. Observe how students are doing, giving assistance as needed.

Step 5

Ask students to put the ropes down. Explain to the students that they are going to add jumping. Ask, "Who remembers what part of their body bends when jumping?" Then ask students to watch and copy. Get in the ready-to-jump position as before (put your hands in front of your body at waist level), but this time bend your knees and ankles. Have students copy. Ask students to do this movement several times, adding their words to the movement and adding the word JUMP when they jump. Students might be using the words READY, DOWN, AROUND, JUMP as they do the movement. You can participate or watch and observe.

Step 6

Ask students to pick up their ropes and try to jump rope using the learner SAY & DO they just practiced.

Facilitation and Reflection

Ask students the following questions to help them reflect on their experiences and extend their thinking:

- *Why is learning to jump rope hard?*
- *What do you need to do to jump more than one or two times?*

20

Space Exploration

Students explore the concepts of spatial awareness through moving their bodies in personal and general space.

Essential Question

When we are moving our bodies, what must we remember about the space around us?

Curriculum Concepts

- Space awareness — personal space; general space
- Locomotor movement
- Nonlocomotor movement

Physical Education National Standard(s)

Standard 2

Materials

- Poly spot (flat, polyvinyl circle)
- Carpet square
- Number on court for each student
- Drum

Steps to Success

Step 1

Ask students the essential question "When we are moving our bodies, what must we remember about the space around us?" and have a discussion with the class.

Ask students to try different ways to move their body in the space provided (e.g., jump on the number, skip around poly spot). Walk around and provide language by labeling the movements the students are performing.

Step 2

Ask for volunteers to share with the class their favorite movement from Step 1. For example, Sarah jumped up and down on her poly spot. Have the class try Sarah's movement. Add labels to Sarah's movement, for example, saying JUMP, JUMP, JUMP, JUMP. Have several more students perform their movement and have the class copy each movement and add the label.

Step 3

Ask students what they noticed about the space they used around them when moving their bodies in different ways. Students might say something like, "I went around my spot" or "I stayed on my spot." Ask the students how they were able to avoid touching anyone while they were moving. When explaining the space they move their bodies in without touching others, label it as "personal space" (enough space to explore and move comfortably without bumping into others).

Step 4

Ask students to try different ways to move their body as they move around the play area (gym, classroom, court, grassy area).

Step 5

Ask students what happened as they tried to move around the play area. Susie might say she bumped into Kelly when she was skipping. When explaining the space they share with others as they travel around the play area, label it as "general space."

Step 6

Have students explore different ways they can move in general space. Ask them to notice what they might have to do with their bodies to keep from bumping into others.

Step 7

Ask for volunteers to share their general-space movement as the rest of the class copies. Label the movement. (Examples might include running, jumping, galloping, or skipping.) Have several other students share their movement and have the class copy.

Step 8

Ask students what they did to keep from bumping into one another while traveling in general space. (Students may say something like, "Slowed down" or "Went around them.")

Facilitation and Reflection

Ask students the following questions to help them reflect on their experiences and extend their thinking:

- *How do you know if you have enough room in your personal space?*
- *What do you know about moving in general space?*

Extensions

Reduce the amount of general space in which students can move. Have students continue to try to move safely without touching others. Reduce the available general space again. Bring to students' awareness how they are changing their body movements as the general space gets smaller.

21

Striking Balloons

Each student has a balloon and explores different ways to strike the balloon while using different body parts. Students gain an understanding of timing, force, and visual tracking during this activity.

Essential Questions

What is striking (hitting)?

What is a pattern?

Curriculum Concepts

- Manipulative skill — striking
- Timing
- Visual tracking
- Force

Physical Education National Standard(s)

Standards 1, 2

Materials

- Inflated balloons (one for each student)

Steps to Success

Step 1

Ask students the essential question "What is striking (hitting)?" Define striking and discuss the concepts mentioned by the students. Students might say, "It is when you hit something."

Step 2

Give each student a balloon. Remind students to get in their own space (personal space) where they have plenty of room to move and not interfere with other students. Have students explore striking the balloon while using different body parts and while trying to stay in their personal space. Tell students that they can use their elbows, head, fingers, nose, and feet to strike the balloon. After they have had time

Striking Terms

Striking — Having the striking surface at the right place at the right time to make contact.

Timing — The coordination and regulation of movement needed to achieve the desired effect; in the example form this lesson, the timing required to make contact with an object.

Visual tracking — Following an object with your eyes.

Force — The capacity to work or cause physical change; strength; power. In this case, how hard an object is hit or struck.

to experiment, have students take turns sharing with the class how they were striking their balloon. Ask students how they were able to stay in their personal space.

Step 3

Ask students what visual tracking has to do with striking. Discuss with them the definition of this term and how you have to use your eyes to watch and follow the object to be able to strike it with accuracy (relating visual tracking to striking).

Step 4

Ask students to use learner SAY & DO as they strike their balloon. That is, students find a way to strike the balloon and then say the body part they are using to hit the balloon. For example, if a student is using his head to strike the balloon, he will say HEAD every time the balloon touches his head. Have students share how they used learner SAY & DO. The class will copy the leader.

This student gains experience with timing and visual tracking as she strikes a balloon with her elbow.

Step 5

Review the definition of patterns. Have students explore making AB patterns while using learner SAY & DO. An AB pattern is one that alternates two things, such as red, white; red, white; and so on. An example of an AB movement pattern that a student might use in this activity with learner SAY & DO would be alternating touching her elbow and her head while naming which part she is touching: ELBOW, HEAD; ELBOW, HEAD; and so on. Have students take turns sharing their AB patterns with the class. Be sure to have students try out the different patterns.

Step 6

Ask students, "Why is force important when striking continuously?" Students use light force when striking a balloon continuously. This practice allows them to answer the question.

Have students get a partner and teach each other their AB pattern. Remind the students that a pattern keeps repeating.

Facilitation and Reflection

Ask students the following questions to help them reflect on their experiences and extend their thinking:

- *What did you find out about timing when you were striking the balloon?*
- *What did you find out about force?*
- *How did you use visual tracking when you were striking the balloon?*
- *How did you use learner SAY & DO?*
- *How did you use patterns today?*

Extensions

Second grade extension:

After Step 5, have students join another person and make sets of partners (four students in each group). Have the partners put their AB patterns together using learner SAY & DO. Each group will decide what type of pattern they have now.

For example, students get into pairs and strike one balloon back and forth across a line using learner SAY & DO. This may also involve a striking pattern. For example, Claire and Kay may strike the balloon across the line using their feet while saying the word KICK. Austin might use the pattern HAND, FOOT to get the balloon across the line, while Greg might use the pattern ELBOW, HEAD to get the balloon across the line.

22

Symmetrical and Asymmetrical Shapes

Students explore making symmetrical and asymmetrical shapes with their bodies.

Essential Question

What do you know about symmetry?

Curriculum Concepts

- Relationships between parts of the body and self — symmetrical and asymmetrical
- Nonlocomotor movement

Physical Education National Standard(s)

Standards 2, 5

Materials

- Visual of objects that are symmetrical (e.g., a butterfly, a bird flying with wings extended, soldier standing at attention) and asymmetrical (Statue of Liberty, flowers, trees, a soldier saluting)
- Cards of stick figures (showing symmetrical or asymmetrical poses; see reproducible examples at the end of this activity)

Steps to Success

Step 1

Ask students the essential question "What do you know about symmetry?" Discuss definitions of *symmetrical* and *asymmetrical* with visuals.

Symmetry Terms

Symmetrical — Both sides of the body are positioned in exactly the same way. For example, a student might put both arms out in front of his body with palms facing up.

Asymmetrical — Each side of the body is positioned differently. For example, a student might put one arm above his head and the other arm down by his side.

Step 2

Have students explore making symmetrical and asymmetrical shapes with their bodies. Encourage students to share by being the leader as the class copies and labels the leader's shape.

Step 3

Ask students to find a partner. First, the leader makes a symmetrical or asymmetrical statue and the partner copies the statue and labels the statue as either symmetrical or asymmetrical. The partner then changes the statue to make it asymmetrical if it was originally symmetrical, or symmetrical if it was originally asymmetrical. For example, Becky made a statue with her arms straight above her head. Her partner, Olivia, made the same symmetrical statue and then she changed it by putting one arm down to her side, leaving one arm straight above her head. Olivia turned Becky's symmetrical statue into an asymmetrical statue.

Leaning back on one arm, this student makes an asymmetrical shape with his body.

Step 4

Students change partners and individually try out different nonlocomotor movements at the same time. They decide together whether each nonlocomotor movement is symmetrical or asymmetrical. Each pair shares a movement with the class, and the class copies. The class decides whether the nonlocomotor movement is symmetrical or asymmetrical.

Step 5

Students change partners again and individually try out different locomotor movements at the same time. They decide together whether the locomotor movements are symmetrical or asymmetrical. Pairs share with the class and the class copies the movements.

Facilitation and Reflection

Ask students the following questions to help them reflect on their experiences and extend their thinking:

- *What did you find out about symmetrical and asymmetrical body shapes?*
- *Thinking about sports skills, pick a skill and label it symmetrical or asymmetrical.* For example, kicking a soccer ball is asymmetrical, and doing a handstand on a mat is symmetrical.
- *In what other subjects might you have to understand the concept of symmetry?* Students may talk about subjects such as math, art, or music.

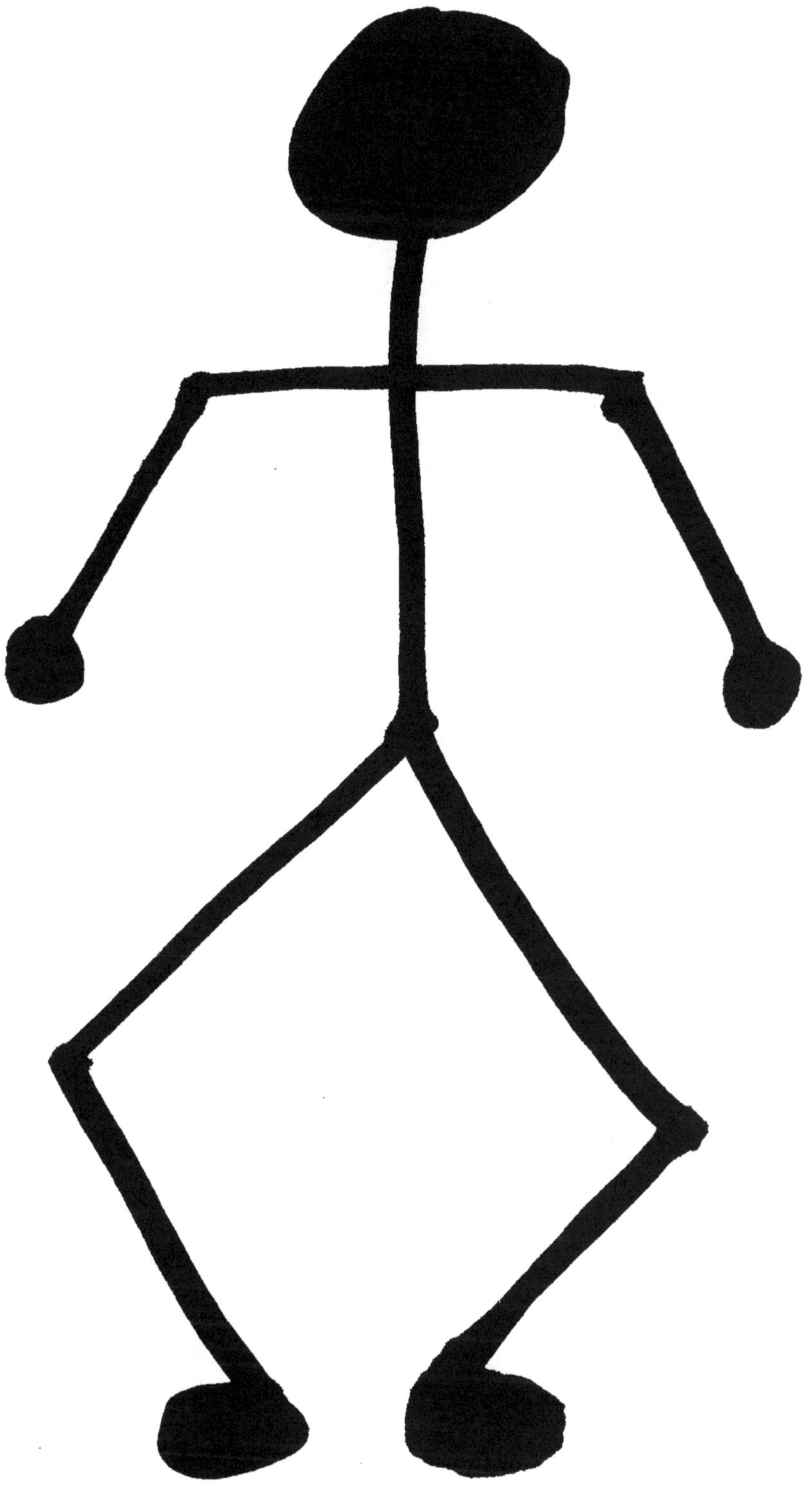

23

Time: Fast or Slow?

Students explore all the ways they can move their bodies fast or slow in personal and general space.

Essential Questions

How can we move our bodies fast? How can we move our bodies slow?

Curriculum Concepts

- Body awareness — time (fast, slow)
- Spatial awareness — personal space; general space
- Building vocabulary

Physical Education National Standard(s)

Standards 1, 2

Materials

- Hand drum
- Recordings "Gaelic Waltz" and "Popcorn" (on accompanying CD)

Steps to Success

Step 1

Ask students the essential questions "How can we move our bodies fast? How can we move our bodies slow?" Ask students to get in their personal space to explore moving their body slowly. Walk around, commenting and providing language for the movements individual students are trying out. Also ask students what they are doing to make their body move slowly.

Step 2

Repeat Step 1 using fast movements. *Note:* The movements are in the students' own timing. However, you could decide to use a hand drum to set the timing for the movements.

Step 3

Ask students to explore moving slowly in general space. Ask for students to share their slow movements with the class as the class copies. Take as many volunteers as possible. Make note of the different levels the students may be using. (For example, "Linda is crawling slowly at a low level. LeJohn is marching very fast, at a high level.")

Step 4

Ask students to explore moving fast in general space. Ask the students what they discovered when they were moving fast. Ask questions that encourage students to compare and contrast their slow and fast movements.

Step 5

Ask students to name a locomotor movement. For example, a student says "walking." Start walking slowly and ask the students to join you and try walking slowly. Then stop and ask the class to try walking fast. Together with the class, try another locomotor movement, first doing it slowly and then doing it faster. After trying that movement together, ask students to try out other locomotor movements in slow and fast time.

Step 6

Ask students what they discovered when trying different locomotor movements in slow and fast time.

Step 7

Ask students to find a partner. In each pair, have one student lead a movement in slow time as the partner copies. The student copying the leader labels the movement and describes the movement he or she did. Then students switch roles.

Step 8

Have student pairs repeat Step 7 with movements in fast time. Have students switch roles.

Step 9

Have students think of action words that describe moving fast and slow. Write some of the words on the board or on paper. Ask students to put movement to the words. Examples of action words include *pounce, sneak, dash, dart, slither,* and *creep.*

Facilitation and Reflection

Ask students the following questions to help them reflect on their experiences and extend their thinking:

- *What do you now know about fast and slow movements?*
- *Name some times when we should move slowly.*
- *Name some times when we should move fast.*
- *What might be some consequences of using the wrong speed during certain times of the school day?*

Extensions

Use words to describe ways to move at various speeds. Examples of words that could be used in sentences include *fast, run, gallop, stomp, dash, spin, explode, jerk, pounce, skip, dart, slow, walk, step, tiptoe, crawl, slither, float, melt, push, creep,* and *sneak.* Suggest to students that they could make a story from their sentences.

Use music for creative movement in fast and slow time. For slow time you could use "Gaelic Waltz" (on accompanying CD), and for fast time you could use "Popcorn" (on accompanying CD).

24

Weight Transfer Sequences

Students explore different ways to transfer weight while using different body parts. Students use different weight transfers and balances to create a sequence.

Essential Question

What does it mean to transfer weight from one part of our body to another?

Curriculum Concepts

- Weight transfers to other body parts
- Sequences

Physical Education National Standard(s)

Standards 2, 5, 6

Materials

- Mats

Steps to Success

Step 1

Ask students the essential question "What does it mean to transfer body weight?" Discuss as a group the answers given by students, and describe taking weight off of one body part and putting the weight on a different body part. Include words that you will use during this lesson (see the sidebar, right). For example, try to bring out the words *sequence* and *balance*.

Step 2

Discuss safety guidelines the students need to remember when working on mats. For example, be sure to remind students that only one person can be on the mat at a time.

Terms for Weight Transfer Sequences

Static balance — This involves maintaining a desired shape in a stationary position. Examples might include handstands, headstands, and gymnastic balances.

Dynamic balance — This involves maintaining an on-balance position while moving, starting, and stopping. Example of a dynamic balance is running, skipping, and other locomotor movements.

Weight transfer — This involves taking weight from one body part and putting it on another.

Step 3

Warm up and stretch with students.

Step 4

Ask students to explore taking weight on various body parts other than on their feet. Ask students to take turns sharing their idea with the class. Ask all students to copy and talk about where they are taking weight. For example, Marcus decided he was going to take weight on his knees. All of the students copied Marcus by putting their knees on the mat. Have other students share their ideas.

Step 5

Have students explore rolling, then ask for volunteers to show how they were rolling. Have the students talk about how they felt their weight being transferred when they were rolling.

Step 6

Ask students to relate dynamic balance to weight transfer: Have students practice their weight transfers while staying balanced. For example, Tania transferred weight from one knee to the other knee without falling.

Step 7

Have students plan a sequence of weight transfers, one of which must be a static balance. A student might plan to balance on one foot, follow this with a forward roll, and then do a cartwheel. Have students label the parts of their sequences. Labels for the example above would be "static, dynamic, dynamic."

This student is transferring his weight from his hands to his knees.

Step 8

Have students share their planned sequences with the class, with a partner, or with you. Have students label the parts of their sequences and discuss how they transferred weight.

Facilitation and Reflection

Ask students the following questions to help them reflect on their experiences and extend their thinking:

- *What did you find out about transferring weight to body parts other than your feet?*
- *When might you have to do this?* For example, when you get out of a swimming pool, you transfer weight to your hands, then to your feet as you get out of the pool.
- *Which balances were harder or easier?*
- *Why is it important to stay balanced?*

25

Words Are Where?

Students reinforce the knowledge of position words while using their bodies.

Essential Question

What are position words (words that tell *where*)?

Curriculum Concepts

- Relationships with objects and/or people
- Position words
- Writing sentences

Physical Education National Standard(s)

Standards 1, 2

Materials

- Hula hoop for each student

Steps to Success

Step 1

Ask students the essential question "What are position words?" Give a visual example (put hula hoop over your head). Ask students to copy and describe the relationship of the hoop to their own bodies. Students might say something like, "The hoop is over my head" or "The hoop is in my hands."

Give a different visual example and have the students copy the movement. Ask the students "where" the hoop is in relationship to something or someone else. Ask students to use position words such as *beside, under, inside, outside, on,* or *off*. The words they use will vary depending on the visual example you have given them.

This student practices holding his hoop in different positions in relation to his body.

Step 2

Have students explore movements with a hula hoop and brainstorm position words they can show with their hoop. For example, Kara is tiptoeing around the hoop; Jacob is holding his hoop between his knees; Sondra is holding her hoop up above her head; and Blake is running around his hoop. Have students take turns sharing with the class as everyone else in the class copies.

Step 3

Ask students to create a sentence to describe their movement using position words (this can be the same movement they made up in Step 2 or a different one). For example, "I am hopping *inside* the hoop," or "My arms are *around* the hoop." Have students share their movement with the rest of the class as they say their sentence. The other students will copy the leader's movement while they repeat the leader's sentence.

Facilitation and Reflection

Ask students the following questions to help them reflect on their experiences and extend their thinking:

- *When do we use position words in physical education?*
- *When do we use position words in the classroom?*
- *Why would it be important to understand position words?*

Extensions

For first and second grades:

Students can create sentences and movements that contain multiple position words.

Activities for Grades 3-5

1

Around and Around

Students experience moving in nonlocomotor ways while stretching different body parts.

Essential Questions

What is flexibility?

What are nonlocomotor movements?

Curriculum Concepts

- Flexibility
- Nonlocomotor movements
- Relationships with objects or people, in the sense of going around
- Spatial awareness

Physical Education National Standard(s)

Standards 1, 2, 5

Materials

- Yarn balls, 1 per student
- 1 die per pair of students

Steps to Success

Step 1

Ask students the essential questions "What is flexibility? What are nonlocomotor movements?" and discuss each with the class.

Step 2

Have students think about safety issues for being inside the classroom. Review safety guidelines.

Step 3

Ask students to find a safe (personal) space around the room. Give each student a yarn ball. Ask students to explore tossing and catching their yarn ball. Have them add learner SAY & DO words as they do so: TOSS and CATCH. Then ask student volunteers to share how they were tossing and catching the ball. Have the rest of the class watch and copy the movement. Have several other students share their movements as the class watches and then copies.

Step 4

Ask students to watch and copy. Pass a ball *around* your waist several times in transferring the ball from one hand to the other, and back again. Ask students "What movement were we doing?" Go in the opposite direction and add the word PASS. Say the word PASS each time the ball goes from one hand to the other. Talk about learner SAY & DO with students. Ask them "Why is it important to say the words while you are doing the movement?"

Step 5

Ask students to explore different ways they can move the ball *around* different parts of their body. After a few minutes, have students add a word/label to the movement.

Step 6

Ask for a student to share how he or she moved the ball around his or her body. Have the rest of the class watch and then try the movement, adding the word the leader used. Have several students share their ideas as the class copies.

Step 7

Have students find a partner (someone near them). Give each pair of students a die. First, the leader rolls the die and decides what movement he or she will do (repeating the movement the number of times shown on the die). The leader shows his or her partner the movement and says the label that goes with it (e.g., "Diamond rolls a 5." The leader moves the ball around her knee five times saying KNEE, KNEE, KNEE, KNEE, KNEE. She said "knee" because that was the body part she chose to move the ball around.

These students choose to move the ball around their knees the number of times shown on the die they rolled.

Step 8

Partners switch — the other person rolls the die, chooses a movement and labels, and shares with the partner.

Facilitation and Reflection

Ask students the following questions to help them reflect on their experiences and extend their thinking:

- *How did you work together today to be successful with your movements?*
- *How did you stretch your body?*
- *How does stretching lead to flexibility?*

Extensions

- After each person has a turn, before they roll the die again, have the students put their movements together to build a pattern/sequence).

2

Balance That Math

Students experience balancing on different body parts while learning about multiplication products.

Essential Questions

What do you know about static and dynamic balance? What do you know about multiplication products?

Curriculum Concepts

- Static balance
- Dynamic balance
- Products — multiplicands and multipliers
- Extension — quotients (divisor and dividend)

Physical Education National Standard(s)

Standards 1, 2, 5

Materials

- Pair of dice for each set of partners

Steps to Success

Step 1

Ask students the essential questions "What do you know about static and dynamic balance? What do you know about multiplication products?" (See the sidebar, right.) The teacher and students in the class discuss the answers to the questions.

Step 2

Ask students to explore representing numbers doing static balances. For example, Rena might stand on one foot. She is representing the number 1. Have students share their ideas with the rest of the class as the other students copy the leader.

Activity Definitions

Static balance — This balance involves maintaining a desired shape in a stationary position. Examples might include handstands, headstands, and gymnastic balances.

Dynamic balance — This balance involves maintaining an on-balance position while moving, starting, and stopping. Examples of a dynamic balance include running, skipping, and other locomotor movements.

Multiplication product — This is the number or quantity obtained by multiplying two or more numbers together.

Step 3

Ask students to explore dynamic balances. Examples of dynamic balances include jumping, running, or walking. Ask students to share their dynamic balances with the class as the other students copy the leader.

Step 4

Ask students to find a partner, and give each person a die (one die from a pair of dice). Each partner in each pair rolls his or her own die to determine the number of body parts he or she will use to create a static balance. The number of body parts being balanced will represent a set of numbers to be multiplied that was determined by the roll of the dice. Together the partners will work to figure out the product of the numbers determined by each of their separate rolls of the dice. Students roll the dice several times, coming up with various combinations. For example, Jim rolled a "3," and Carmen rolled a "4." For that combination, the pair has to represent a balance with 12 body parts on the floor. See the photo on page 7 for an example.

Step 5

Have the partners repeat the process described in Step 4 while using dynamic balances. For example, Juan rolls the number 6 and his partner, Ben, rolls the number 3. The product of 6 and 3 is 18, and so they do 18 locomotor movements to represent the product (e.g., 10 jumps and 8 marches).

Step 6

Have students work together, repeating the process in Steps 4 and 5 while using a combination of static and dynamic balances. For example, Jody rolls a 6 with her die and Jessica rolls a 5. The partners calculate that the product of these two numbers is 30, and they choose to represent 30 by doing 20 gallops and then balancing on 10 body parts total between the two girls.

Step 7

Ask students to put the dice away and find a different student to be their partner. Give each pair a product, for example, the number 18. Have students think of all the combinations of numbers that can be multiplied to equal 18. Have partners pick two combinations to represent with a static or dynamic balance. Have student pairs share their balances with the entire class.

Facilitation and Reflection

Ask students the following questions to help them reflect on their experiences and extend their thinking:

- *What did you find out about representing products with static and dynamic balances?*

Extensions

- Steps 2–6 could be used to reinforce the concepts *greater than* and *less than*. Have partners roll their die, and after they each create their static or dynamic balance to represent the number on the die, they can make a statement like *"Seven is greater than three,"* or *"Four is less than five,"* or *"Two is equal to two."*
- Steps 2–6 could also be used to reinforce division.

3

Basketball – Shooting

Students explore different techniques for shooting a basketball. The teacher and students use learner SAY & DO to work on the elements of shooting.

Essential Question

What do you know about the technique of shooting a basketball?

Curriculum Concepts

- Manipulative skill — shooting a basketball

Physical Education National Standard(s)

Standards 1, 2

Materials

- Basketball for each student

Steps to Success

Step 1

Ask students the essential question "What do you know about the technique of shooting a basketball?" and have a class discussion.

Step 2

Have students get a basketball and explore using different techniques to shoot the basketball in personal space (students are not shooting into basketball goals but are pretending to shoot in personal space). Ask for volunteers to share the techniques they used and have the rest of the class copy. Ask for other volunteers to share as the class copies.

Step 3

Ask students to describe what they have to do with their bodies to shoot a basketball. Students' answers may include "Shooting with one hand," "One hand is my guide hand," "Elbow pointing to the goal," "Ball above my eyes," "Had to jump in the air," "Bent my knees," "Feet shoulder-width apart," "Elbow bent," and so on.

Step 4

Have the students watch and copy as you put the basketball in your dominant hand in shooting position and hold the ball above your eyes. After students copy, also have them try their other hand.

With guidance from the teacher, this student explores different ways of shooting a basketball.

Step 5

Have students practice movement without the ball using learner SAY & DO. Have students put their own words to the movements of their arm and wrist (e.g., EXTEND, PUSH). Have students watch as you shoot the ball in the air in your personal space (pretend shooting at a basketball goal); allow the ball to bounce; catch it, and repeat.

Step 6

Have the students practice shooting with the ball using learner SAY & DO. Remind students to also try shooting with their other hand. (*Note:* Some students may not be able to balance the ball with one hand.) Ask students what happens with their nonshooting hand. Ask students to add their guide hand (the nonshooting hand that helps guide the ball as one shoots with the other hand) to help hold the ball in place.

Step 7

Ask students what happens to the ball as it rolls off their fingertips when pushed during shooting. Ask students what parts of their body help when shooting. Have the class try shooting using their legs — remind students that bending their knees and using their legs to lift their body off the floor is very important when shooting. Students are still shooting in the air in personal space, not at a basketball goal. Ask for a student volunteer to demonstrate a jump shot. Have the rest of the class copy and try to add jumping to their shooting.

Facilitation and Reflection

Ask students the following questions to help them reflect on their experiences and extend their thinking:

- *What are the critical elements of shooting?* Students' answers might include "Elbow in line with the shoulder pointing to the goal," "Ball on fingertips — not palm of the hand," "Ball above the eyes," "Fingers push the ball," "Follow-through," "Jump," or "Use guide hand."

Extensions

- Have students aim at targets on the wall or backboard without goal so they can concentrate on technique.

4

Bele Kawe (BAY-luh KAH-wee)

This is an African dance from the Caribbean Island of Carriacou. This dance can be done in a circle or in free formation with no hands held. This dance includes locomotor and nonlocomotor movements and works on balance, body awareness, and space awareness. This dance also requires right- or left-foot correctness. Be sure to check out the foot used for each movement under the beat boxes.

Essential Question

What is a weight transfer?

Curriculum Concepts

- Locomotor movement
- Nonlocomotor movement
- Balance
- Body awareness
- Space awareness
- Basic timing
- Sequencing

Physical Education National Standard(s)

Standards 1, 2

Materials

- Recording of "Bele Kawe" (on accompanying CD)

Steps to Success

Step 1

Ask students the essential question "What is weight transfer?"

Step 2

Perform the following dance steps to "Bele Kawe" with students.

Language-to-Dance Vocabulary

IN: Moving toward the center of the circle

OUT: Moving away from the center of the circle

CLOSE: Stepping next to the foot that has moved side, or in, or forward

TOUCH: A movement of the foot against the floor

HEEL: A movement placing the heel on the floor

TURN: Turning the body on the step to face a different direction

SIDE: Moving sideward while facing center (toward the circle)

JUMP: Landing on both feet at the same time

CW: Clockwise — the direction the circle is moving

Part IA

IN / OUT	CLOSE	IN / OUT	CLOSE	IN / OUT	CLOSE	IN / OUT	CLOSE
R L	R	L R	L	R L	R	L R	L

Repeat

Beats 1: Step R foot in with bent knees (males with backs of hands on hip pockets, females hold long skirts).

&: Step L foot out.

2: Step R foot next to L foot.

3–4: Repeat beats 1–2 with opposite footwork.

5–16: Repeat Parts IA, beats 1–4, three more times.

> **Dance Notation for Left Foot and Right Foot**
>
> When you see the left-foot notation, L, or the right-foot notation, R, in parentheses — (L) or (R) — that means you are using the left or right foot, as indicated, and that it is a nonlocomotor movement.

Part IA (simplified)

IN	TOUCH	OUT	TOUCH	IN	TOUCH	OUT	TOUCH
R	(L)	L	(R)	R	(L)	L	(R)

Repeat

Part IB

HEEL	OUT	HEEL	OUT	HEEL	OUT	HEEL	OUT
(R)	R	(L)	L	(R)	R	(L)	L

HEEL	IN	HEEL	IN	HEEL	IN	HEEL	IN
(R)	R	(L)	L	(R)	R	(L)	L

Beats 17: Touch R heel diagonally sideward right (arms extended sideward, elbows slightly bent).

18: Step R foot slightly out.

19: Touch L heel diagonally sideward left.

20: Step L foot slightly out.

21–24: Repeat beats 17–20.

25–32: Repeat Parts IB, beats 17–24, moving in.

To Simplify: 8 steps OUT, 8 steps IN.

Part II

CCW				CW			
HEEL	IN	HEEL	IN	HEEL	IN	HEEL	IN
R	L	R	B	L	R	L	B

Repeat

Beats 1–2: Step R, L foot turning right a full wide turn (hands behind back, elbows sideward, body bent slightly forward).

3: Step R foot sideward right.

4: Jump with feet apart (the jump is the male's part; females rest on beat 4 and may shake shoulders).

5–8: Repeat beats 1–4, turning left beginning with L foot.

9–16: Repeat Parts II, beats 1–8.

To Simplify: Step in place or walk forward without the TURN or TURN but omit JUMP; add REST on beat 4. No R foot or L foot needs to be specified, if dance is simplified.

Lead-Up Activities: Practice a rocking motion of IN, REST, OUT, REST then IN, TOUCH, OUT, TOUCH (at individual tempo). Have students practice walking OUT and IN in a 2-beat sequence using a TOUCH before the STEP. TOUCH on beat 1 and STEP on beat 2 (individual tempo). Have students practice turning right and left in 3 steps with a REST on the fourth beat (individual tempo). Add a JUMP on beat 4 after the turns are comfortable.

Teaching Suggestions: Part I — Using learner SAY & DO, use the simplification IN, TOUCH, OUT, TOUCH until students are able to do the IN/OUT, CLOSE successfully. Have students practice 4 HEEL, OUT steps followed by 4 HEEL, IN steps. HEEL, OUT is much more difficult because the foot is moved farther following the TOUCH of the heel. Have students practice the transition of the IN, TOUCH, OUT, TOUCH to the HEEL, OUT (the TOUCH to the HEEL is difficult). Have students perform all of Part I with group SAY & DO Part II. Have students practice the transition from the final JUMP to IN, TOUCH at the beginning. Use learner SAY & DO through the entire dance, and then add the music.

Facilitation and Reflection

Ask students the following questions to help them reflect on their experiences and extend their thinking:

- *What sequence of movements did you find to be the hardest? Why?*
- *What sequence of movements did you find to be the easiest? Why?*

Extensions

Chair Dancing (to do with students seated in their chairs)

Part I: Have students do beats 1–16 as described. Have them do the HEEL, OUT and HEEL, IN in place or begin with the feet away from the chair in order to move them toward and away from the chair.

Part II: Have students do 3 steps in place and add a JUMP motion of both feet.

5

Building Sequences Using Locomotor Movement

Students use locomotor movement to design, develop, and perform movement routines (sequences).

Essential Questions

What is locomotor movement?

What is a sequence?

Curriculum Concepts

- Locomotor movement
- Timing (steady beat)

Physical Education National Standard(s)

Standards 1, 2

Materials

- Recording of "Blackberry Quadrille" (found on accompanying CD)

Steps to Success

Step 1

Ask students the essential questions "What is locomotor movement? What is a sequence?" and review students' knowledge of these concepts.

Step 2

(As a warmup)

Ask students to explore different locomotor movements. Ask for a volunteer to demonstrate his or her favorite movement and have the class copy. Go through all locomotor movements. Allow students to suggest several examples of locomotor movements and try them out.

Step 3

Have students listen to a musical recording. Ask the students if they noticed when the music changed. Ask students to choose two different locomotor movements to use with the music. Ask students how they changed the locomotor movement when the music changed. Also ask students what in the music made them change their movement. Students might say, "I had to speed up or slow down my movement to fit the music," or "I was moving on every beat of the music."

Step 4

Ask students to make a plan to use two locomotor movements to the same music. The students may choose to use the same movement as they did in Step 3 or they can choose two different movements.

Each time the music changes the students should change the locomotor movement.

Step 5

Have students choose a partner with whom to share their sequence of locomotor movements, as done in Step 4. Students may find that using the learner SAY & DO strategy would be helpful in this activity. Each partner shares his or her locomotor movement sequence. After each partner knows the other's sequence, the pair puts the movements together to form a sequence of four movements. For example, Pat's sequence was *march, hop*. Mark's sequence was *jump, gallop*. When they put the four movements together they were doing *march, hop, jump, gallop*. Each time the music changed, students changed the movement. The students marched 16 beats, hopped 16 beats, jumped 16 beats, then galloped 16 beats.

Have the partners try the sequence of four movements without the music. When everyone feels comfortable, add the music.

These student partners share their locomotor movement sequences.

Step 6

Have students create *new* movement sequences using four different locomotor movements.

Facilitation and Reflection

Ask students the following question to help them reflect on their experiences and extend their thinking:

- *What did you discover about putting locomotor movements to music?* Students might say that some movements fit better with the music than did others, or they might comment that they had to think about which movement to do first so they could change to the second movement more easily. You may hear some students say that they prefer to hear the music before planning the movements in the future.

Extensions

- Have partners pick another set of partners with whom to combine their movements to make a sequence of 8 movements.

6

Close Encounters*

"Close Encounters" is a dance from the United States, and the music used for this dance is called the "California Strut." This is a partner dance with partners standing side by side facing counterclockwise. There is a 16-beat introduction.

Essential Question

What do we need to remember when working together with a partner?

Curriculum Concepts

- Locomotor movement
- Nonlocomotor movement
- Basic timing
- Sequencing
- Space awareness

Physical Education National Standard(s)

Standards 1, 2, 5

Materials

- Recording of "California Strut" (on accompanying CD)

Steps to Success

Step 1

Ask students the essential question "What do we need to remember when working with a partner?"

Language-to-Dance Vocabulary

FWD: Forward — Dancers move one behind the other around the circle or in a line

BWD: Backward — Dancers move one behind the other around the circle or in a line

TOUCH: A movement of the foot against the floor

AROUND: A step on the designated foot to begin a sequence of steps that travel around a partner, as in a do-si-do.

CW: Clockwise — The direction the circle is moving

CCW: Counterclockwise — The direction the circle is moving

Step 2

Perform the following dance steps to "California Strut" with students:

CCW

FWD	FWD	FWD	KICK	BWD	BWD	BWD	TOUCH
L	R	L	(R)	R	L	R	(L)

Repeat

Beat 1: Step L foot forward counterclockwise.
2: Step R foot forward counterclockwise.
3: Step L foot forward counterclockwise.
4: Kick R foot forward counterclockwise.
5–8: Repeat Part I, beats 1–4, moving backward beginning R foot (clockwise); beat 8, touch toe in back.
9–16: Repeat Part I, beats 1–8, and turn to face partner (inside person has back to center of circle).
To Simplify: Omit the kick and touch.

Note: To increase complexity in Part I, move sideward right and left, beats 1–8.

AROUND (DO-SI-DO)	2	3	4	5	6	7	8
L	R	L	R	L	R	L	R

CCW

HIT	HIT	BUMP	BUMP	FWD (CHANGE)	FWD	FWD	FWD
				L	R	L	R

Beats 17–24: Do-si-do 8 steps (partners pass R shoulders then move back to place, passing L shoulders).
25–26: Partners "high-five" hands 2 times.
27–28: Partners bump hips (each partner uses his or her hip to make contact with one of the other partner's hips) 2 times.
29–32: Inside person walks 4 steps forward counterclockwise to new partner; outside person turns clockwise 4 steps or steps in place 4 steps.

Note: No R foot or L foot needs to be specified for any of the dance steps.

Lead-Up Activities: Using learner SAY & DO, have students step in place 3 steps and balance on fourth beat, then step in place adding KICK and TOUCH (individual tempo). Finally have students change to FORWARD, FORWARD, FORWARD, KICK, and BACKWARD, BACKWARD, BACKWARD, TOUCH (individual tempo). Review or teach a do-si-do.

Teaching Suggestions: Have partners practice beats 1–16 with partner SAY & DO (each partner uses learner SAY & DO), then group SAY & DO (everyone in the group uses learner SAY & DO). Have partners practice transition from beat 16 to the do-si-do. Have partners do the sequence HIT, HIT, BUMP, BUMP, then SAY & DO. Have partners SAY & DO beats 17–32, adding the change of partners.

Facilitation and Reflection

Ask students the following questions to help them reflect on their experiences and extend their thinking:

- *What sequences were used in this dance?*
- *How did you and your partner have to work together?*

Extensions

- Have the partners explore other movements and develop a dance to this piece of music. Be sure the students are using the strategy of learner SAY & DO. Use the reproducible blank beat box form found in Appendix A.

**Choreographed by Phyllis S. Weikart*

Students dance with a partner in "Close Encounters."

GRADE: 3–5

7

Creating Group Routines

Students experience weight transfers, balance, and symmetry while working in a group to plan a group routine.

Essential Questions

What do you know about weight transfers? About balance? About symmetry?

Curriculum Concepts

- Inverted balance
- Weight transfers to body parts other than hands
- Symmetry

Physical Education National Standard(s)

Standards 1, 2, 6

Materials

- Mats
- Paper
- Pencil

Steps to Success

Step 1

Ask students the essential questions "What do you know about weight transfers? About balance? About symmetry?" Ask students to review with a partner their knowledge about balance, symmetry, and weight transfer. Have a group discussion about these concepts.

Step 2

Introduce or review inverted balances. Discuss the concept of synchronization and cooperation. (See the sidebar, right, for definition.)

Moving With Purpose

Inverted balance — A balance done upside down using any combination of equal weight on the hands, head, one foot, shoulders, or arm.

Synchronization — Two or more people organizing their movements to look identical.

Step 3

Ask students to get in groups of four and go to a mat. Discuss the classroom safety rules the students should follow while on the mats.

Step 4

Warm up and stretch together with students, going through several exercises. A warm-up session might include jogging for one minute; doing a shoulder stretch (across the chest); doing a side stretch (oblique); resting the head on one shoulder and then the other (neck stretches); stretching quad muscles by bending one knee and holding it with the hand on the same side of the body, standing on the other foot; doing a "butterfly" stretch by having the bottom of the feet touching while seated on the floor with knees pointing out to the side; and doing toe touches.

Step 5

Students explore all kinds of inverted balances (balances that require your head, knees, hands, back of head, shoulders, arms, or one foot to take weight equally, such as a headstand); static balances (maintaining a desired shape in a stationary position, such as standing on both feet with arms up in the air); dynamic balances (occurring in a weight transfer — these could include jumping, throwing, catching, and all forms of locomotor movement); symmetrical body shapes (both sides of the body doing exactly the same thing, as in a hand stand); and asymmetrical body shapes (where one side of the body is doing something different from the other side of the body, such as a balance with both feet on the floor and one hand on the floor with the other hand up in the air). Students take turns sharing their ideas with the class as the class copies the leader and labels the different skills demonstrated. For example, Jonathan might share a balance that has his head and both hands on the floor, with his elbows on his knees. Marijata copies and says it is a "triangle." You say the name of Jonathan's pose is a *tripod* because he is balancing with his weight on three body parts.

Step 6

Have students get in pairs and practice synchronizing a skill with each other. For example, Jill and Molly try synchronizing a cartwheel together. Have students share how they worked together to synchronize their movements. For example, Jill and Molly put words to the sequence of movements they had to use to perform the cartwheel. The words they used were APPROACH, TAKEOFF, OVER, UP. Please remember that it is very important to allow students to come up with the words they need to use to synchronize their own movements.

Step 7

Have students get in groups of two, three, or four and plan a group routine. Each routine must include the following:

- A weight transfer from feet to hands
- An inverted balance
- A roll
- A symmetrical and asymmetrical body shape (see pp. 97–98)

Students coordinate their movements in a group routine as they transfer their weight from their feet to their hands.

Step 8

Have the students in each group put their routines together by showing the movement first with no language and then performing the movements again and adding learner SAY & DO. Once everyone in the group has shared the movement, practice synchronization by adding learner SAY & DO.

Step 9

Have students share their group routine with the class.

Facilitation and Reflection

Ask students the following questions to help them reflect on their experiences and extend their thinking:

- *Which balances and weight transfers were easiest? Which were harder?*
- *What did you find out about trying to synchronize your movements with other students?*
- *When have you seen people synchronize their movements?*

Extensions

For fifth grade:

- The concept of counterbalance may be included for fifth-grade students. An example of counterbalance is when a student stands on one foot and holds his arms straight out to each side while extending the free leg. This is counterbalance because the arms and the free leg are extended in opposite directions.

Note: Routines can be videotaped and shown to students for self-assessment.

8

Creating Step Routines

Students work with locomotor and nonlocomotor movements to create step routines.

Essential Question

What is the difference between locomotor and nonlocomotor movement?

Curriculum Concepts

- Locomotor movement
- Nonlocomotor movement
- Timing
- Sequencing

Physical Education National Standard(s)

Standards 1, 5, 6

Materials

- Aerobic steps for each student
- Recording of "Rakes of Mallow" (on accompanying CD)

Steps to Success

Step 1

Ask the essential question "What is the difference between locomotor and nonlocomotor movement?" Have a class discussion on this topic. Also ask "What is a 4-beat movement pattern?" "What is learner SAY & DO?"

Step 2

Have students explore ways to move on and off their aerobic fitness step. For example, one student may step on and off the step, and another student may step on the step and then step off the step from the side or the front. See the photo on page 17 (left) for an example. Have students take turns sharing their movements as the rest of the class copies.

Step 3

Have each student create a 4-beat movement pattern on and off the step using learner SAY & DO. For example ON, KICK, OFF, OFF. In this example, the person steps on with one foot, kicks with the other foot, steps off with the kicking foot, and then steps off with the foot that was on the step.

Ask for volunteers to share as the rest of the class copies the pattern. Have students label which part(s) of the pattern are locomotor and which are nonlocomotor movements.

Step 4

Have students try repeating a 4-beat movement pattern four times while using learner SAY & DO in their own timing. That is, their movements are timed to the rhythm of the words they say.

Step 5

Have two students share their 4-beat movement pattern as you write their patterns in beat boxes on the whiteboard. For example

Austin

ON	ON	OFF	OFF

4X

Laura

ON	KICK	OFF	OFF

4X

Perhaps you have students try Austin's pattern four times followed by Laura's, also four times. Have the class use learner SAY & DO. First each student tries the pattern using his own timing and then the entire class tries the pattern, saying and doing the pattern together. Have the class try the pattern to music.

Step 6

Have students work in pairs or small groups to create a step routine of two or four 4-beat patterns. Have students practice in unison in their groups. Have students practice with WHISPER & DO when using the music. Have students share routines with the class. (*Note:* You can find a reproducible blank beat-box form in Appendix A.)

Facilitation and Reflection

Ask students the following questions to help them reflect on their experiences and extend their thinking:

- *What did you find out about creating locomotor and nonlocomotor 4-beat movement patterns while using the aerobic fitness steps?* Students may give answers like "I had to be careful with the movements I put together," or "When I tried to add words I had to change my movement to make it work."
- *How could this activity relate to aerobic capacity?* Aerobic capacity is the capacity of the body's respiratory and cardiovascular systems to transport oxygen to working muscles.

Extensions

- Have students go back to the routines they created and add arm movements to their steps. This will make the activity much more difficult because they will be using integrated movement.

9

Different "Swings" With a Racket

Children explore striking with a racket, using a shuttlecock (birdie).

Essential Question

What factors affect striking?

Curriculum Concepts

- Manipulative skill — striking
- Spatial awareness — space for striking
- Visual tracking

Physical Education National Standard(s)

Standards 1, 2

Materials

- Badminton or tennis rackets (one per student)
- Shuttlecocks (one per student)

Steps to Success

Step 1

Ask students the essential question "What factors affect striking?" Ask students to explore all the different ways they can swing their racket. Have students label how they are swinging (e.g., *overhand, underhand, forehand, backhand*).

Step 2

Give each student a birdie. Ask students to try striking the birdie using all of the different ways they can swing their racket. See the photo on page 17 (right) for an example.

Step 3

Ask someone to share how he or she was striking the racket and birdie. Have the rest of the class copy the student leader's way of striking. Ask students what determines how the birdie travels after being hit (e.g., the kind of swing, force, speed). Ask for another student to share his or her idea as the class copies. Ask students to compare and contrast the two ways of striking. Ask if any other students want to share.

Note: If this is the first time students are using these rackets, the exploration of different ways to strike and swing may take longer.

Step 4

Have students watch and copy you as you show them how to transition their body (turn side to target) for a forehand swing. Pull your arm back to swing the racket forward. Ask students to explore hitting the birdie in a forward direction using a sidearm swing.

Step 5

Have students watch and copy as you show them how to transition (side to target) their body for a backhand swing. Pull your arm back to swing the racket forward. Ask students to practice striking the birdie in a forward direction using a backhand sidearm swing.

Step 6

Ask students if they have discovered what concept most affects their ability to strike the birdie.

Step 7

Follow Steps 4 and 5 to give students practice with the overhead swing. Have students watch and copy you as you show them how to transition their body (turn side to target) for an overhead swing. Hold the racket above your head, pull your arm back to swing the racket forward, and follow through with a downward motion.

Step 8

Follow Steps 4 and 5 to give students practice with the underhand swing. Have students watch and copy you as you show them how to transition their body (turn side to target) for an underhand swing. Hold the racket with your palm turned up. Pull your arm back to swing the racket forward, and follow through with the arm and racket coming upward.

Facilitation and Reflection

Ask students the following questions to help them reflect on their experiences and extend their thinking:

- *What concepts affect striking?*
- *How is striking like throwing?*

Extensions

- Set up targets (e.g., cone, hula hoop, carpet square) and have students work toward accuracy in hitting the target with a birdie.
- Have students get into pairs and strike an object (e.g., birdie, foam balls, balloons, ping-pong balls) back and forth to each other. The students try to keep the object in the air. Encourage students to use different types of swings with the racket.

10

Dribble – Knock Away

Students use the skill of dribbling to control their own ball while trying to knock other students' balls away.

Essential Question

What are the critical elements of dribbling?

Curriculum Concepts

- Manipulative skill — dribbling
- Offensive and defensive strategies
- Space awareness
- Body awareness

Physical Education National Standard(s)

Standards 1, 2, 6

Materials

- Basketball for each student
- Markers, such as cones or poly spots, if you do the activity extension given on page 128.

Steps to Success

Step 1

Ask the essential question "What are the critical elements of dribbling?" and have a class discussion on this topic.

Step 2

Have each student get a basketball and find a personal space. Have students explore dribbling in their space. (Remind students to explore dribbling using one hand and then the other).

Step 3

After a few minutes, have the students stop dribbling. Ask them to think about what they might do to keep someone from knocking the ball away from them. Have the students try out some of the strategies they thought about. Ask for student volunteers to share their ideas as the rest of the class copies the volunteer's idea.

Have students come up with strategies for protecting their ball while dribbling, such as keeping their knees bent, using the hand that is not dribbling as a shield, keeping their body between the ball and the other person, and keeping their head up and eyes focused on where they want to travel.

Step 4

Let the students know they are going to play a game called Knock Away. Tell them they will need to use defensive strategies (trying to take the ball away from another) and offensive strategies (trying to keep the ball from being taken away) to play the game.

Explain that on a signal everyone will begin to dribble. Say that each person will try to keep dribbling his or her own ball and move to try to knock someone else's away from them — using the hand they are not using to dribble their own ball — and that the goal is to not let one's own ball get knocked away. Explain that, if a student's ball gets knocked away, the student retrieves the ball and joins back in the game.

Together with a few students, demonstrate the game for the rest of the class.

Step 5

Ask the class to find a personal space in which to start. They will do this in an overall space you have defined that is large enough that students with limited skill can still be successful at this point in the lesson but small enough that students have to use offensive and defensive skills.

When everyone is ready, give the start signal for the game to begin. The signal can be whatever you usually use in class.

Step 6

After a short time, have the students stop. Students retrieve their balls and find a personal space in which to start the game again.

Facilitation and Reflection

Ask students the following questions to help them reflect on their experiences and extend their thinking:

- *What was the most challenging part of the "Knock Away" game? Why?*
- *Were there any new offensive or defensive strategies you tried or learned today concerning dribbling?*

Extensions

- As students' skill level improves, reduce the amount of space in which the students have to dribble. Use cones, poly spots, or other markers to define the space.

11

Dribbling to a Steady Beat

Students combine information they know about dribbling and steady beat to develop dribbling sequences to a steady beat.

Essential Questions

What do you know about dribbling? What do you know about steady beat?

Curriculum Concepts

- Manipulative skill — dribbling
- Timing
- Force

Physical Education National Standard(s)

Standards 1, 2, 6

Materials

- Basketball or other type of ball that will bounce, one for each student
- Music: "Soldier's Joy" (included on accompanying CD); "Peat Fire Flame" (included on accompanying CD); you may also want to get a recording of "Sweet Georgia Brown" (not included on accompanying CD)

Steps to Success

Step 1

Ask students the essential questions "What do you know about dribbling? What do you already know about steady beat?" Answers to the question about dribbling should include the critical elements of dribbling such as using fingertips on the ball, keeping the ball under the waist, keeping knees bent, keeping eyes forward, and having a firm wrist. Talk with students about these elements.

Ask students what they know about steady beat. Answers from students might include "Same speed," "Stays the same," "Keep it steady," or "Doesn't change."

Step 2

Have students get a basketball and find their own personal space. Have students explore dribbling, trying to keep in mind the key elements listed in Step 1.

Step 3

Have students take turns being the leader and sharing their dribbling and timing. For example, Mark might share how he was dribbling with his left hand and how his timing was very slow. Monica might share how she dribbled her basketball back and forth in front of her while alternating hands as she dribbled very fast. Have the other students in the class copy the leader's dribbling and try to match the leader's speed.

Step 4

After several students have shared their ideas, add a strategy: While asking the students to use learner SAY & DO, tell them that each time the ball hits the floor, they will say BOUNCE. This strategy allows all students to get and stay together in the same timing, working on beat awareness and developing timing.

Step 5

Have students get in groups of three to five and try using the learner SAY & DO strategy as they take turns leading a dribble. Each leader decides on the type of dribble and sets the timing by dribbling the ball at a steady tempo. All the other students in the group copy the leader.

Step 6

Students will listen to a musical recording such as "Soldier's Joy" or "Peat Fire Flame." While the students are listening to the music, they will keep steady beat to the music without the ball. For instance, students might pat the beat on their knees or shoulders, or march to the music using their feet.

Step 7

Restart the music (at the beginning, including the introduction) and have students dribble their basketball to the beat of the music, trying to keep the beat steady.

Step 8

Have students get back into their previous groups (see Step 5) and develop a dribble sequence by putting together their ideas for dribbling. Each student will choose a way to dribble the basketball, and together the students will determine who will go first, second, third, and so on. Have students practice without the music first. Then put the

Students gain awareness of steady beat as they dribble their basketballs to the beat of the music.

music back on (at the beginning) and have students try out their dribbling sequence to the music. Groups discuss with the rest of the class how their dribbling sequence worked with the music. Ask students "Did you have to change your plan or order of the sequences?"

Facilitation and Reflection

Ask students the following questions to help them reflect on their experiences and extend their thinking:

- *What are the critical elements of dribbling?*
- *How did adding music make the dribbling easier or harder?*
- *How did your group decide the order of the dribbling sequence?*

Extensions

- In Step 8, play a variety of music selections to which students can try out their dribbling sequence. Have the students discuss what happened to their sequence when the music selection was slower or faster.

12

Dribbling With Feet

Students experience dribbling with their feet, which reinforces the concepts of force and balance.

Essential Question

What is dribbling?

Curriculum Concepts

- Manipulative skill — kicking
- Timing
- Force
- Balance

Physical Education National Standard(s)

Standards 1, 2

Materials

- Soccer balls, one for each student
- Recording of "La Raspa" (on accompanying CD)

Steps to Success

Step 1

Ask students the essential question "What is dribbling?"

Step 2

Have each student get a soccer ball and explore tapping it back and forth between their feet while staying in personal space.

Step 3

Discuss the parts of the feet used to dribble. Ask students to think about the amount of force needed to control the ball. Demonstrate "toe taps": putting one foot on top of the ball and switching feet quickly.

Learning to switch feet quickly and tap the ball with the right amount of force is part of learning to dribble a soccer ball.

Step 4

Have students explore toe taps at their own pace. Ask "What do you need to do toe taps quickly?" Students may answer "Balance," "Light force on the ball," or "Strength."

Step 5

Play the recording of the musical piece "La Raspa" (found on the CD in the back of this book). This recording has an AABB form of music. During the first two sections (AA) of the music, the students will perform toe taps. During the B sections of the recording, students will tap the ball back and forth between their feet using light force.

Turn the music on and demonstrate this sequence of movements to the recording. Have students listen to the music and join you in the movements when they are ready.

Facilitation and Reflection

Ask students the following questions to help them reflect on their experiences and extend their thinking:

- *How do the concepts of force, timing, and balance affect dribbling?*
- *Why are "quick" feet important when dribbling?*

Extensions

- Instead of staying in personal space and tapping the ball back and forth as in Step 5, have the students travel while dribbling during the B section of the musical recording "La Raspa."

13

Face-Off

Students use basic striking skills (dribbling) to gain control of the ball or hockey puck from their partner and maintain control for a short period of time.

Essential Question

What do you know about striking (dribbling) with a hockey stick?

Curriculum Concepts

- Manipulative — striking with long-handled implement
- Offensive and defensive strategies
- Space awareness
- Body awareness

Physical Education National Standard(s)

Standards 1, 2, 6

Materials

- Hockey stick for each student
- Hockey puck or whiffle ball for each student

Steps to Success

Step 1

Ask the essential question "What do you know about striking with a hockey stick?" and have a class discussion on this topic.

Step 2

Have students get a hockey stick and ball, and tell them to find a personal space. Ask students to think about safety issues for using the hockey sticks. Review the safety rules.

Step 3

Ask the students to explore the skill of dribbling using a hockey stick. Then ask for student volunteers to share how they were dribbling with their hockey stick. Perhaps Randy was jogging and he changed direction three times while dribbling the ball with the hockey stick. Have the class copy his example. Ask other students to share their way of dribbling as the rest of the class joins in.

Step 4

Ask the class to describe what happens to get a hockey game started. Have students find a partner or else you can put students in pairs. Have one partner in each pair put his or her ball or puck away.

Step 5

Tell students they are going to play Face-Off. Have partners face each other with the ball or puck on the ground between the hockey sticks. Tell students that on the start signal, each pair of students will battle to gain control of the puck or ball. The student gaining control will use offensive strategies and dribbling to maintain control of the ball or puck and keep it away from his or her partner. The student who doesn't gain control of the ball or puck must use defensive strategies to try to gain possession of the ball or puck.

Together with a student, demonstrate how the game works, including use of offensive and defensive strategies.

Step 6

Have the students play Face-Off. Stop the game after a few minutes. Then have students regroup (get back in position across from their partners) for another round of the game.

Facilitation and Reflection

Ask students the following questions to help them reflect on their experiences and extend their thinking:

- *Why is the skill of dribbling so important in hockey?*
- *What was the most challenging part of the Face-Off? Why?*

Extensions

- Put two sets of partners together to make four in a group. Have students begin Face-Off in the same way, but now each person has a player on his or her team to whom he or she can pass the ball or puck. Have students take turns being the Face-Off person. The Face-Off person for each team is the person who is trying to gain control of the puck for that team.

GRADE: 3–5

14

Fjäskern* (f-YESS-kern) – Hurry Scurry

Use this dance to get your students out of their seats and get their heart rate up. The dance is from Sweden, and it starts off slow and then gets faster and faster. The dance uses all locomotor movements. The formation for this dance is a single circle facing counterclockwise. This dance has an 8-beat introduction, and no specific foot is required.

Essential Question

When you are in a hurry, how does your body move differently?

Curriculum Concepts

- Locomotor movement
- Space awareness
- Body awareness
- Basic timing
- Sequencing

Physical Education National Standard(s)

Standards 1, 2, 4

Materials

- Recording of "Fjäskern" (on accompanying CD)

Steps to Success

Step 1

Ask students the essential question "When you are in a hurry, how does your body move differently?"

Step 2

Perform the following dance steps to "Fjäskern" with students.

Language-to-Dance Vocabulary

FWD: Forward — Dancers move one behind the other around the circle or in a line

SCISSOR: A forward kicking movement of the legs in which the kicks occur in sequence — one leg kicks forward while the weight is brought down on the other foot, under the body

TURN: Turning the body on the step to face a different direction

CCW: Counterclockwise — the direction the circle is moving

CW: Clockwise — the direction the circle is moving

Part I

FWD	FWD	FWD	FWD	FWD	FWD	FWD	FWD
R	L	R	L	R	L	R	L

2X CCW, 2X CW

Beats 1–16: Walk 16 steps forward counterclockwise, turning on the final step to face clockwise.

17–32: Walk 16 steps forward clockwise, then partners turn to face each other on the final step.

Part II

SCISSOR	SCISSOR	SCISSOR	SCISSOR	TURN (CHANGE)	TURN	TURN	TURN
R	L	R	L	R	L	R	L

4X

Beats 1–4: Leap 4 times (straight up in the air and back down in place), alternating feet; extend the nonweight-bearing heel to the floor in front of the body.

5–8: Step 4 times, changing places with one's partner; clap with the first word, TURN and pass R shoulders

9–32: Repeat Part II, beats 1–8, three more times

Part II (simplified)

SCISSOR	SCISSOR	SCISSOR	SCISSOR	IN (CLAP)	IN	IN	IN
R	L	R	L	R	L	R	L

SCISSOR	SCISSOR	SCISSOR	SCISSOR	OUT (CLAP)	OUT	OUT	OUT
R	L	R	L	R	L	R	L

REPEAT Part II (SIMPLIFIED)

Beats 1–4: Repeat Part II, beats 1–4, in place, facing center.

5–8: Step 4 times, moving to the center of the circle; clap with the first word IN.

9–16: Repeat beats 1–8, moving away from the center of the circle.

17–32: Repeat Part II (simplified), beats 1–16.

Note: No R or L foot needs to be specified.

Lead-Up Activities: WALK counterclockwise then clockwise in a continuous movement (individual tempo). SCISSOR 4 times then WALK forward 4 steps (individual tempo, then match the tempo of your partner)

Teaching Suggestions: Teach the simplified version first. Change Part II to the partner version. Have students practice using the partner beat then using group SAY & DO. Add music.

These students move clockwise in a circle while dancing Fjäskern.

Facilitation and Reflection

Ask students the following questions to help them reflect on their experiences and extend their thinking:

- *What happened to the speed of the dance?*
- *What did you have to do with your body to keep up with the music?*

Extensions

- Have students get in groups and make up new movements that can be used to this piece of music. Use the original dance and an example. Use the reproducible blank beat box form found in Appendix A.

15

Fitness Ball

Students use throwing and catching skills as they move in personal space.

Essential Question

What does fitness mean?

Curriculum Concepts

- Manipulative skills — throwing/catching
- Cardiovascular fitness
- Space Awareness (inside classroom)
- Locomotor movements

Physical Education National Standard(s)

Standards 1, 2, 4, 6

Materials

- Soft (e.g., foam) ball (6–8 in.; one ball for the whole class)

Steps to Success

Step 1

Ask the essential question "What does fitness mean?" and discuss with class.

Step 2

Ask students to think about safety issues for being inside the classroom. Review classroom safety guidelines with the students. Have students stand behind their desk or move to safe (personal) space.

Step 3

Inform students that the game they will be playing uses the skills of throwing and catching. Ask students to show different ways they might throw or catch a ball. Call out different things you see the students doing as they throw and catch (e.g., "I see overhand throws," "I see underhand throws," "I see students catching with one hand," etc.).

Step 4

Also explain to the students that the game uses different locomotor movements that can be done in personal space. Ask student volunteers to demonstrate a locomotor movement in personal space as the class watches and copies. Review all locomotor movements that can be done in personal space.

Step 5

Discuss the rules for the game as they are listed below. Allow students to change and make up different rules as they get more comfortable playing the game.

Rules for the game:

1. Throwers are standing, and they must make accurate throws to their target (another person).
2. Catchers are standing, and they must catch the ball that comes to them.

Note: You or the students may add or change rules; for example, you might invent a rule that could be stated *You cannot throw the ball back to the person who threw it to you;* or a rule that could be stated *The ball must be passed boy-girl-boy-girl. Consequence: If you break the rules you are out (temporarily) of the game and sit on the floor or in a chair for a minute or two, observing so as to understand the rules and strategies of the game.* Note that, with the last rule, sitting out for a few minutes is not meant to be a punishment, but an opportunity for students who need more processing time to understand the game.

Students practice throwing and catching skills as they play Fitness Ball in the classroom.

Step 6

To warm up, have the students stand in place to play. This allows students to get an understanding of the game.

Step 7

After a few minutes, stop the game and tell the students the group is adding another movement to the game: they must *jog* in place while playing. Let students who were out come back into the game. Start the game again.

Step 8

Let students suggest different locomotor movements to use in the game. Students stay in their personal space as they perform the movements.

Step 9

Students who get out can "earn" their way back into the game by doing a certain number of pushups or sit-ups. Students may choose another activity, such as jumping jacks.

Facilitation and Reflection

Ask students the following questions to help them reflect on their experiences and extend their thinking:

- *What did you find out about throwing and catching while you played Fitness Ball?*
- *How could this game affect your fitness?*

Extensions

- Bring students' attention to the concept of heart rate. You could use heart rate monitors or have students count their own pulse to find a target heart rate. (See p. 55 for a discussion of heart rate.)
- Students can wear pedometers during this activity to track the number of steps taken during the game.

GRADE: 3–5

16

Hacky Sack

Students explore using hacky sacks to increase eye-foot coordination, balance, and timing.

Essential Question

What is a hacky sack?

Curriculum Concepts

- Manipulative skills — kicking/striking
- Space awareness (inside classroom)

Physical Education National Standard(s)

Standards 1, 2, 5

Materials

- Hacky sack, one per student

Steps to Success

Step 1

Ask students the essential question "What is a hacky sack?" Also ask students if they have used one before and discuss their experiences.

Step 2

Ask students to think about safety issues for being in the classroom. Review classroom safety guidelines with the students.

Step 3

Hand out hacky sacks to all students and ask them to find a safe personal space.

Step 4

Ask students to explore striking/bouncing the hacky sack using their hands and arms.

Step 5

Ask for volunteers to share how they were striking the hacky sack. For example, Tony bounces the hacky sack on the back of his hand. The rest of the class watches and then tries Tony's idea. Ask for several students to share while the rest of the class copies.

Step 6

Ask students to watch and copy as you use the inside of your foot to kick the hacky sack up into the air and catch it in your hand. Explain that this is one way to use the hacky sack with your feet. Have students explore other ways they can use their feet to kick the hacky sack. Repeat the Step 5 process.

Step 7

Ask students to find a partner. Challenge students to find a way to keep the hacky sack going between themselves and their partner, using only their feet. Ask for pairs to volunteer to share how they were trying to keep the hacky sack going back and forth. Have the rest of the class watch and try out their ideas. Ask if any others want to share.

Students reinforce their eye-foot-hand coordination as they practice kicking the hacky sack into the air and catching it in their hand.

Facilitation and Reflection

Ask students the following questions to help them reflect on their experiences and extend their thinking:

- *What did you learn about using hacky sacks?*
- *How did the amount of space you had to work within affect your successful use of the hacky sacks?*

Extensions

- Put two sets of partners together to make a group of four and repeat Step 7.

17

The Hustle

The Hustle is a dance from the United States and is performed in a free formation. It includes locomotor and nonlocomotor movements. This dance requires balance.

Essential Question

What is a weight transfer?

Curriculum Concepts

- Locomotor movement
- Nonlocomotor movement
- Basic timing
- Space awareness
- Sequencing

Physical Education National Standard(s)

Standards 1, 2, 6

Materials

- Recording of "The Hustle" (found on accompanying CD)

Steps to Success

Step 1

Ask students the essential question "What is a weight transfer?"

Step 2

Perform the following dance steps to "The Hustle" with students.

Language-to-Dance Vocabulary

FWD: Forward — moving one behind the other around the circle or in a line

TOUCH: A movement of the foot against the floor

BWD: Backward — moving one behind the other around the circle or in a line

JUMP: Landing on both feet at the same time

HOP: Landing on one foot

FWD	FWD	FWD	TOUCH	BWD	BWD	BWD	TOUCH
L	R	L	(R)	R	L	R	(L)

FWD	FWD	FWD	TOUCH	TOUCH	TOUCH	TOUCH	TOUCH
L	R	L	(R)	(R)	(R)	(R)	(R)

TOUCH	TOUCH	TOUCH	STEP	TOUCH	TOUCH	JUMP (¼ TURN)	HOP
(R)	(R)	(R)	R	(L)	(L)	B	R

Beats 1–3: Step L, R, L foot forward.
4: Touch R foot forward.
5–7: Step R, L, R foot backward.
8: Touch L foot backward.
9–12: Repeat beats 1–4.
13–16: Touch R foot forward twice then backward twice.
17–20: Touch R foot forward, backward, sideward, then step next to L foot.
21–22: Touch L foot sideward, touch L foot next to R foot.
23: Jump, turning ¼ left.
24: Hop R foot bringing L foot up in back.

Note: Dance may be simplified by not specifying R or L foot.

Lead-Up Activities: Practice balancing on one leg and touching the free foot in front, in back, to the side, etc. (individual tempo). Practice FORWARD, FORWARD, FORWARD, TOUCH; BACKWARD, BACKWARD, BACKWARD, TOUCH (individual tempo). Practice TOUCH 3 times followed by a STEP (individual tempo). Practice JUMP, HOP executing a 1/4 TURN (individual tempo).

Teaching Suggestions: Begin with the first 12 beats and keep adding on the next section of 4 beats. Use individual tempo, then group SAY & DO. Practice the transition from the end to the beginning. SAY & DO the entire dance and then add the music.

Facilitation and Reflection

Ask students the following questions to help them reflect on their experiences and extend their thinking:

- *What movements in this dance used weight transfers?*
- *What movements did not use weight transfers?*

GRADE: 3–5

18

Irish Stew*

This is a two-part dance from the United States. The musical recording is a melody from Ireland called "Rakes of Mallow." This dance gives students the opportunity to practice movement sequences to music composed of locomotor and nonlocomotor movements. The dance formation is a circle, without hands joined. You do not need to specify whether to use the right or left foot. There is an 8-beat introduction.

Essential Question

What is a sequence?

Curriculum Concepts

- Locomotor movement
- Nonlocomotor movement
- Basic timing
- Sequencing

Physical Education National Standard(s)

Standards 1, 2

Standard 6 (Extension)

Materials

- Recording of "Rakes of Mallow" (on accompanying CD)

Steps to Success

Step 1

Ask students the essential question "What is a sequence?" Have a discussion.

Step 2

Perform the following movements to "The Rakes of Mallow" with children.

Language-to-Dance Vocabulary

FWD: Forward — moving one behind the other around the circle or in a line

IN: Moving toward the center of the circle

OUT: Moving away from the center of the circle

JUMP: Landing on both feet at the same time

CCW: Counterclockwise — the direction the circle is moving

CW: Clockwise — the direction the circle is moving

Introduction: Students rest for 8 beats.

Part I

FWD	FWD	FWD	FWD	FWD	FWD	FWD	FWD
R	L	R	L	R	L	R	L

2X CCW, 2X CW

Beats 1–16: Locomotor movement counterclockwise (walk or use variations).
17–32: Repeat locomotor movement clockwise.

Part II

JUMP	JUMP	CLAP	CLAP	JUMP	JUMP	CLAP	CLAP
B	B			B	B		

IN	IN	IN	IN	OUT	OUT	OUT	OUT
R	L	R	L	R	L	R	L

Repeat Part II

Beats 1–2: Jump 2 times (in place, apart-together, or scissor fashion).
3–4: Clap hands 2 times.
5–8: Repeat beats 1–4.
9–12: Step R, L, R, L foot toward the center.
13–16: Step R, L, R, L foot away from the center.
17–32: Repeat Part II, beats 1–16.

Lead-Up Activities: Practice different locomotor and nonlocomotor sequences.

Teaching Suggestions: This type of two-part music gives students the opportunity to practice many sequences to music, alternating locomotor and nonlocomotor movements.

Facilitation and Reflection

Ask students the following questions to help them reflect on their experiences and extend their thinking:

- *What were the sequences used in this dance?*
- *What was the hardest part of the dance? Why?*

Extensions

- Have students explore other locomotor or nonlocomotor movements that would work in place of the ones in the original dance. Put the music back on and let students try out their new movements to the music. Use the reproducible blank beat box form found in Appendix A.

**Choreographed by Phyllis S. Weikart*

GRADE: 3–5

19

Les Saluts (lay sah-LEU)

This is a French Canadian dance, and it uses all locomotor movements. During the dance the students are required to move in several directions to the beat of the music. The dance is done in a circle with or without hands joined. It has a very short introduction of 4 beats.

Essential Question

What do you have to do with your body to change directions quickly?

Curriculum Concepts

- Locomotor movement
- Balance
- Basic timing
- Space awareness
- Sequencing

Physical Education National Standard(s)

Standards 1, 2

Materials

- Recording of "Les Saluts" (on accompanying CD)

Steps to Success

Step 1

Ask students the essential question "What do you have to do with your body to change directions quickly?"

Step 2

Perform the following dance steps to "Les Saluts" with students.

Language-to-Dance Vocabulary

FWD: Forward — moving one behind the other around the circle or in a line

IN: Moving toward the center of the circle

OUT: Moving away from the center of the circle

CCW: Counterclockwise — the direction the circle is moving

CW: Clockwise — the direction the circle is moving

Part I

FWD	FWD	FWD	FWD	FWD	FWD	FWD	FWD
R	L	R	L	R	L	R	L

2X CCW, 2X CW

Beats 1–16: Walk 16 steps counterclockwise.
17–32: Walk 16 steps clockwise.

Note: To give students additional experiences, vary the WALK or use other locomotor movements; no R foot or L foot needs to be specified.

Part II

IN	IN	IN	IN	OUT	OUT	OUT	OUT
R	L	R	L	R	L	R	L

IN	IN	IN	𝄐 (BOW)	OUT	OUT	OUT	OUT
R	L	R	L	R	L	R	L

Beats 1–4: Walk 4 steps in.
5–8: Walk 4 steps out.
9–12: Walk 3 step in and bow; hold bow until music begins again
13–16: Walk 4 steps out.

Note: Fermata 𝄐: keep bowing as long as music indicates.

Lead-Up Activities: Have students experiment with locomotor movements. Have students practice walking to the steady beat of music: they practice walking IN 4 steps then walking OUT 4 steps.

Teaching Suggestions: Practice Part II with learner SAY & DO, then add music. Practice Part I with music.

Facilitation and Reflection

Ask students the following questions to help them reflect on their experiences and extend their thinking:

- *What did you have to do to prepare to change direction?*
- *What part of the dance was the hardest place to balance your body?*

20

Name That Game

Students use an overhand throw to develop/design a throwing/catching game.

Essential Question

What do you know about throwing a football?

Curriculum Concepts

- Overhand throw
- Catching

Physical Education National Standard(s)

Standards 1, 2, 6

Materials

- Footballs, enough for each pair of students
- Clipboards, enough for each group of four students
- Paper, enough for each group of four students
- Pencils, enough for each group of four students

Steps to Success

Step 1

Ask students the essential question "What do you know about throwing a football?" and discuss critical elements of throwing a football (gripping with the fingers across the laces of the football, using an overhand throwing motion, turning the nonthrowing side of the body toward the target, bending the elbows, and pulling the arm back and swinging the arm forward).

Step 2

Have students choose a partner and get a football. Have them warm up by throwing and catching with a partner.

Step 3

Tell students they are going to design and develop a game using the football and an overhand throw. They will need to create rules and directions for how to play their game. You can give them a rule or parameter they must follow (e.g., each person on the team has to touch the ball or no one can run with the ball).

Step 4

Divide the class into groups of four or let students choose their own groups. Send each group to an area with materials (footballs, clipboards, paper, and pencils) to complete the assignment given in Step 3.

Step 5

Visit each group to observe and help the groups get started. Encourage groups to design and develop the game first, then play it to see how it works. After groups have developed their game, have them write down the game rules on paper and give the game a name.

Step 6

Ask each group to share their game with the whole class by demonstrating it and talking about it as they are doing it.

Facilitation and Reflection

Ask students the following questions to help them reflect on their experiences and extend their thinking:

- *What did you discover when trying to make up your game?*

Extensions

- Have students play their game with the same group, using a different type of object (ball) to throw. Have them try several different types of balls.
- Have the different groups try out each other's games.

GRADE: 3–5

21

Nonlocomotor Movement Sequences

Students use nonlocomotor movement to develop, design, and perform movement routines (sequences).

Essential Questions

What is a nonlocomotor movement?

What is a sequence?

Curriculum Concepts

- Nonlocomotor movement
- Timing (steady beat)

Physical Education National Standard(s)

Standards 1, 2, 6

Materials

- Recording of “O'Keefe Slide/Kerry Slide” (on accompanying CD)

Steps to Success

Step 1

Ask students the essential questions “What is nonlocomotor movement? What is a sequence?” and review students' knowledge of these concepts.

Step 2

Have students explore different nonlocomotor movements in their own space. For an example, see the photo on page 39 (left). Ask for a student volunteer to share his or her nonlocomotor movement. Have the class copy the leader's movement. Ask for other volunteers and go through as many nonlocomotor movements as possible.

Step 3

Have students listen to a musical recording. Then ask if they noticed when the music changed. Ask students to choose two different nonlocomotor movements to use with the music. Ask what happened when they changed their movements. Some students might respond that they had trouble changing quickly from one movement to the other, or that the movement didn't really fit the feel of the music. Others might say that the movements they chose didn't work because they didn't go together.

Step 4

Ask students to make a plan to use two nonlocomotor movements to the same music. The students may choose to use the same movement they used in Step 3, or they can choose two different movements. Each time the music changes, the students should change the nonlocomotor movement.

Step 5

Have students choose a partner with whom to share their sequence of nonlocomotor movements done in Step 4. Each partner shares his or her nonlocomotor movement sequence. After each partner knows the other's sequence, the pair will put the movements together to form a sequence of four movements. For example, Sabine's sequence was *twist, shake.* Linda's sequence was *turn, swing.* When they put the four movements together they were doing *twist, shake, turn, swing.* Students may find that using the learner SAY & DO strategy is helpful in this activity.

Have the partners try the sequence of four movements without the music. When everyone feels comfortable, add the music.

Be sure students are performing nonlocomotor movements on the first of every two beats of the musical recording.

Step 6

Have students create a new movement sequence using four different nonlocomotor movements.

Facilitation and Reflection

Ask students the following questions to help them reflect on their experiences and extend their thinking:

- *What did you notice about putting nonlocomotor movements to music?*
- *How is timing different for locomotor/nonlocomotor movements?* Remember locomotor movement is performed on every beat and nonlocomotor movement is performed on the first of every two beats:

Pat		Pat		Pat		Pat	
March	March	March	March	March	March	March	March
Pat		Pat		Pat		Pat	
March	March	March	March	March	March	March	March

Extensions

- Using Steps 2–6 as a guide, have students design a combination of locomotor and nonlocomotor movements to create movement sequences.

22

Parachute Extravaganza

Students work together as one unit to explore different ways to make the parachute move. The students will also move to the music using the parachute.

Essential Question

What do you know about using a parachute?

Curriculum Concepts

- Physical fitness components — muscle strength, endurance, flexibility
- Problem solving
- Timing (steady beat)

Physical Education National Standard(s)

Standards 1, 2, 5, 6

Materials

- Parachute (large enough for entire class)

Or

- Several small parachutes, enough for the number of students in the class
- Different types of balls such as whiffle balls or foam or yarn balls
- Bean bags or rubber animals
- Recording of "Popcorn" (on accompanying CD)

Steps to Success

Step 1

Ask students the essential question "What do you know about using a parachute?" and have a class discussion on this topic. Be sure to include a review of the safety issues in this discussion.

Step 2

Have students spread out around the parachute and explore moving the parachute. After they have picked up the edges of the parachute in their hands, students usually begin to jump up and down and move their arms up and down. After a few minutes, stop the class and ask how they were moving the parachute. At this point the students discover they really can't move the parachute in the way they wanted to move it. Guide a class discussion on cooperation and what needs to happen for the class to be successful in working with the parachute.

Step 3

Ask students how they want to make the parachute move. One student might say he wants "to shake it fast." In this case, then have all the students shake the parachute fast. Another student might say she wants to move the parachute "side to side." Perhaps the students then try to move it side to side, but they discover it doesn't work very well.

The students then have to problem-solve how they are going to have everyone move the parachute to the same side at the same time. Perhaps they decide to put words to the movement. When they do so, they are using the learner SAY & DO strategy. A student may suggest using the words RIGHT and LEFT to keep everyone together.

Continue taking suggestions from the students for how to move the parachute as a group.

Other examples of things students might say to indicate how to move the parachute include "waves," "umbrella," "mountain," "inside mountain," "mushroom," and "floating cloud."

Step 4

Put various pieces of equipment on the parachute, such as foam balls. Have students move the parachute in such a way that the balls pop off the parachute and up into the air.

Step 5

Play a recording of a musical selection such as "Popcorn" (provided on the accompanying CD). Have students choose a locomotor movement that they would like to do to the music while also moving the parachute. For example, the students may decide they want to jump in personal space and move their arms up and down to make the parachute move to the music. Start the music and let students make their movements.

Encourage students to share other ideas of movements that can be done to the music while using the parachute.

Facilitation and Reflection

Ask students the following questions to help them reflect on their experiences and extend their thinking:

- *Why do we use the parachute in our class?* Answers might include "We have to work together to make the shapes," "We are moving the parachute at the same time," and "We are exercising."
- *What are the benefits of using the parachute?*

Extensions

- Use small parachutes in the class and divide the students in groups with about 4–5 students. Have each group develop a routine to music using the parachute. Each group must include nonlocomotor and locomotor movements.
- Many of the recordings found on the CD in the back of this book can be used as the music for this activity. Let the groups choose among several of the musical selections which they would like to move the parachute to.

23

Punting

Students explore punting different kinds of balls. Teacher and students use learner SAY & DO to work on the skill of punting.

Essential Question

What do you know about punting a ball?

Curriculum Concepts

- Manipulative skill — punting
- Timing
- Visual Tracking

Physical Education National Standard(s)

Standards 1, 2, 6

Materials

- Balls of different sizes, shapes, and weights, enough so each student can have a ball of any type
- Other objects for punting (one per student) — for example, beanbags, deflated playground balls, pumpkin balls, etc. (See Appendix D for a pattern for making a pumpkin ball.)

Steps to Success

Step 1

Ask students the essential question "What do you know about punting a ball?" and discuss critical elements of punting (e.g., dropping the ball, having the ball make contact with your shoelaces, keeping your eyes on the ball, swing your kicking foot forward).

What is Punting?

Punting is a way of kicking an object. Punting involves releasing a ball from the hands and kicking it while it is in the air.

Step 2

Place different kinds of balls at different stations (four to five stations, depending on class size). Tell students they will rotate to each station and try punting at each station.

Note: Be sure to talk about safety issues.

Step 3

Divide students equally among the number of stations you have. Have students explore punting. After they have had time to do this, signal for students to stop, put up the balls, and move to the next station. Allow students time to rotate to each station.

This student prepares to punt a pumpkin ball.

Step 4

Ask students what they noticed about trying to punt the balls. Have a class discussion.

Note: You may need to do Steps 5–8 in a subsequent lesson, depending on your students and time issues (or, the entire lesson could be done in one day).

Step 5

Have students get an object or ball different from those used in Steps 1–4 (e.g., beanbag, pumpkin ball, deflated playground ball). Tell students you are going to work on punting using learner SAY & DO, and ask students to watch and copy. As you drop the ball to the ground, say DROP and make sure you drop the ball from waist level using two hands.

Step 6

Have students watch and tell you what they notice as you move your foot and leg: Without the ball, demonstrate kicking with your leg bent back and your foot flexed, and with your toe touching the ground behind you and your weight on your nonkicking leg. You may have to do a static movement and isolate the foot being flexed to help students understand how that movement is done. With your knee bent, swing your leg forward, extending your knee and leg straight in front with toe pointed out. After demonstrating, ask students what they noticed. Have students try the leg movement.

Step 7

Ask students to watch and copy as you do the movement without the object. Begin by pretending to hold the ball out in front of your body, with your arms straight, and letting go of the ball while saying DROP. Your foot will be beginning to swing as you pretend to drop the ball. As your leg and foot become extended, say KICK. All students try punting without using the object.

Step 8

Have students use a ball (or object) with learner SAY & DO to practice punting. Students will say DROP, KICK as they are punting.

Facilitation and Reflection

Ask students the following questions to help them reflect on their experiences and extend their thinking:

- *What are the critical elements of punting?*
- *How did using the learner SAY & DO strategy help you?*

Extensions

- Add targets (hula hoops, cones, markers) as goals for students to use to work on punting for distance, height, and accuracy.
- Have students work in pairs in which they punt to each other to work on punting for accuracy, distance, height, and trying to catch a punted ball.

24

Setting a Volleyball (Overhand Set or Pass)

Students use volleyballs to explore different ways they can set (overhand) a volleyball. They will use learner SAY & DO to work on the skill of setting a volleyball.

Essential Question

What do you know about the overhand set used in volleyball?

Curriculum Concepts

- Manipulative skill — volleying

Physical Education National Standard(s)

Standards 1, 2

Materials

- Volleyballs, one per student

Steps to Success

Step 1

Ask students the essential question "What do you know about the overhand set used in volleyball?"

Step 2

Have each student get a volleyball and find a personal space. Have students explore how to overhand set the volleyball. Have student volunteers share their sets as the class copies. For example, a student might share a set where he is using the palm of his hands. This step allows the teacher to observe students and assess their current level of development in real time.

What Is Overhand Setting?

The **overhand set** is performed with your hands above your head, palms facing toward the ceiling. Using the pads of your fingers, make contact with the ball and push the ball up in the air.

Step 3

Ask students to watch and copy as you hold your hands up overhead with fingers and thumbs touching to form a triangle.

Step 4

Tell students you are going to demonstrate setting the volleyball. Ask them to notice how your body (hands, fingers, eyes, legs) work together to set the ball. Demonstrate.

Step 5

Ask students to discuss what they noticed. Among points to discuss include how your elbows were bent, how the ball hit your fingertips (not the palm of your hand), how your knees were bent, how you kept your eyes on the ball, and how you moved to meet the ball.

Step 6

Have students watch and copy as you put the ball in your fingertips above your eyes. Use your wrist and elbows to push the ball up. *Note:* The ball should land back in your hands where it started.

Step 7

Demonstrate using learner SAY & DO: Toss the ball using two hands (while saying TOSS). Put your hands up and set the ball (say SET). Then catch the ball (say CATCH). Repeat this learner SAY & DO: TOSS, SET, CATCH. Have students join you when they are ready.

Step 8

Show the students continuous setting by using learner SAY & DO: TOSS, SET, SET, SET. Say SET every time your fingers touch the ball. If you lose control, stop and start over.

Facilitation and Reflection

Ask students the following questions to help them reflect on their experiences and extend their thinking:

- *What are the critical elements of the overhand set (pass)?*
- *How did using the learner SAY & DO strategy help you?*

Extensions

- Have students get into pairs. Have one student in each pair toss the ball to his or her partner, who tries to set the ball up in the air; the first partner then catches the ball.
- Have partners try to keep ball going between them using the overhand pass (set) back and forth to each other.
- Put students in groups of three or four. Have students use the skill of setting to keep the ball up in the air continuously or as long as they can as a group.

25

Solving Movement Problems

In this activity, students are going to work with locomotor movements and space awareness concepts. As the students are working, teachers will emphasize students' speaking complete sentences to describe what they are doing.

Essential Question

What do you know about the concepts listed on the poster?

Curriculum Concepts

- Locomotor movement
- Space awareness — levels, directions, pathways
- Body awareness
- Speed

Physical Education National Standard(s)

Standards 1, 2

Materials

- Paper and pencil for each student (used for activity extensions, p. 162)
- Poster you make, using the model below:

Locomotor Movements	Levels	Directions	Pathways	Speed
Walk	High	Forward	Straight	Slow
Run	Middle	Sideward	Curved	Medium
Jump	Low	Backward	Zigzag	Fast
Hop				
Gallop				
Slide				
Leap				
Tiptoe				
Skip				

Steps to Success

Step 1

Ask the essential question "What do you know about the concepts listed on the poster?"

Step 2

Have each student spend a few minutes exploring and deciding on a locomotor movement and combining one or two concepts with that movement. For example, a student may choose to jump in a sideward direction and in a curved pathway. In this example, the locomotor movement is jumping and the concepts are direction and pathway.

Step 3

Have each student create a sentence to describe his or her movements created in Step 2. For example, Jessica might say, "I am going to skip at a middle level in a backward direction."

Step 4

Have students get in pairs. Tell students that one partner in each pair plans a locomotor movement involving other concepts from the poster. The planner carries out his or her plan and the partner copies. After the partner copies, he or she speaks a sentence to describe what his or her partner has performed. Partners take turn being the leaders.

Step 5

Have students change partners; this time, give only verbal instructions to their partner. For example, "Leap at a high level, in a straight pathway, fast."

Facilitation and Reflection

Ask students the following questions to help them reflect on their experiences and extend their thinking:

- *What did you find out about combining concepts?*
- *Which ones were most difficult?*
- *Where else might you have to move in these ways?*

Extensions

- Have students write movement problems on a piece of paper (e.g., tiptoe at a middle level very fast). Have students trade their problems with other students and have them solve the problems.
- Have students share their movement problems with other students and guess what is being left out. In the tiptoeing example given above, the part that was left out was the direction in which the student was moving.

26

Swat That Ball

Students experience striking with a paddle, using foam balls.

Essential Question

What factors are involved in the skill of striking?

Curriculum Concepts

- Manipulative skill — striking
- Force
- Timing
- Visual tracking

Physical Education National Standard(s)

Standards 1, 2

Materials

- Paddles (e.g., foam or lollipop paddles)
- Foam tennis balls

Steps to Success

Step 1

Ask the essential question "What factors are involved in the skill of striking?" and have a class discussion on this topic.

Step 2

Have students explore striking balls with paddles in personal space (as much as is possible; the amount of personal space needed is likely to increase in this activity). Ask students to think about the amount of force that will give them the best control of the paddle and ball. As students are working, have them use learner SAY & DO and ask them to try to think of a word to say as they are hitting the ball with the paddle. For example, one student might say HIT each time he makes contact with the ball.

Have students take turns sharing with the class the way they were striking their ball with the paddle as the other students try to copy. Some students might demonstrate hitting the ball with their paddle turned so their palm is facing up; others might demonstrate hitting the ball on one side of the paddle and then twist their wrist to hit the other side as the ball is coming back down. Ask the students what has to happen to keep the ball in personal space and under control.

Step 3

Have students explore striking with a wall as a target. Then ask students how this striking was different from the way they were striking earlier in this activity.

Step 4

Have students try striking back and forth with a partner using learner SAY & DO. Examples of things students might say while striking include HIT, BOUNCE, HIT, BOUNCE; OR HIT, HIT, HIT, HIT.

Using a lollipop paddle, this student practices hitting a foam ball as many times in a row as he can.

Facilitation and Reflection

Ask students the following questions to help them reflect on their experiences and extend their thinking:

- *How is striking with paddles or rackets different from striking with body parts?*
- *How is striking up or down the same as or different from striking to a wall or to a partner?*
- *How did your timing, force, and visual tracking change as you explored striking with a paddle?*

27

Underhand and Overhand Throwing

Students explore underhand and overhand throwing by throwing the ball against the wall and using the strategy learner SAY & DO.

Essential Question

What do you know about underhand and overhand throwing?

Curriculum Concepts

- Manipulative skills — throwing (underhand, overhand)
- Timing
- Force

Physical Education National Standard(s)

Standards 1, 2

Materials

- Balls
- Wall space if possible (throw to partners if space is not available)

Steps to Success

Step 1

Ask students the essential question "What do you know about underhand and overhand throwing?" Answers from the students might include the concepts of knowing when to let go of the ball (timing), and watching the ball with one's eyes (visual tracking).

Step 2

Have students explore underhand and overhand throwing by throwing their ball against the wall. Have students take turns sharing with the class the way they chose to throw the ball as all of the other students copy the leader. Ask students to talk about the type of throw they were using and describe what their bodies were doing when they were throwing. Ask the students how the movement of their bodies affected the throw.

Step 3

Circulate around the room as the students turn to a partner and choose one of the throws (underhand or overhand) and discuss with them what has to happen for the throw to be a good throw. For example, one student might say, "You can't let go of the ball too late for an underhand throw, or it will go backwards." In this case you might say, "Yes, you have to release the ball at the right time." In this example, the student was learning about timing.

Practicing a right-handed underhand throw, this student steps into the throw with her left foot, which is opposite to her throwing hand.

Step 4

After students have had a chance to explore and discuss the underhand and overhand throw, add in critical elements. Model the following elements as the students copy:

Underhand throw— face toward the target; step into the throw with foot opposite to the throwing hand

Overhand throw— opposite shoulder to the throwing hand faces the target; step into the throw with foot opposite to the throwing hand

Step 5

Have students practice underhand and overhand throws, adding the critical elements listed above. Have the students add the language STEP, THROW to the movements to use the learner SAY & DO strategy.

Step 6

As students continue to practice throwing, add in more critical elements of arm back and follow-through for students to think about as they throw. As students are throwing, draw their attention to bringing their arm back and following through with the arm and hand. (For example, a student may say, TWIST — "My body twists when I throw overhand.")

With his left shoulder facing the target, this student steps into a right-handed overhand throw with his left foot, which is opposite to his throwing hand.

Facilitation and Reflection

Ask students the following questions to help them reflect on their experiences and extend their thinking:

- *What did you find out about timing and force when you were throwing using the critical elements?*
- *What did you notice about the timing once you started to use the learner SAY & DO strategy with STEP, THROW?*

Extensions

- Ask students to choose a partner and practice throwing to each other using the underhand throw.
- Have students move their bodies around so they have to throw the ball at different heights and distances from each other.
- Have students change partners and practice doing the same thing with the overhand throw.
- Discuss how force was being used in each throw.

GRADE: 3–5

28

Underhand Striking (Golf)

Children explore swinging a golf club and experience hitting a ball.

Essential Questions

What do you know about striking? What do you know about striking with a golf club?

Curriculum Concepts

- Manipulative skill — striking
- Visual tracking
- Force
- Timing

Physical Education National Standard(s)

Standards 1, 2, 5

Materials

- Golf clubs (enough for each student, if available, or 1 club for every two students)
- Tennis balls
- Golf mat/tees
- Hula hoops and/or cones

Steps to Success

Step 1

Ask students the essential questions "What do you know about striking? What do you know about striking with a golf club?" Setup: Put tees out in a line across the field about 8 feet apart. At each hitting station (where the tees are placed), put two balls of like color. Make a large landing area 60 feet or more away, opposite the tees. Use targets (e.g., cones, hoops) to make the landing area.

Step 2

Ask students how they might hold (grip) the golf clubs, and simulate swinging the club (underhand swing). The students explore how they swing the club. Volunteers share their experiences with the class.

Step 3

Give a visual demonstration of how to grip using the golf club. Ask students "What other implement uses this kind of grip?" John might answer, "A baseball bat."

Step 4

Have each student get a club and begin to explore gripping and swinging the club (without the ball). Ask students to describe how they are setting up their bodies in order to swing their club toward the tee. Have students take turns sharing their ideas as the rest of the class tries them out.

Step 5

Have students watch and copy as you grip the club in a vertical position with the club head up and grip pointed down. Do this by placing your hand (the closest hand to the target) at the bottom of the grip. Place your dominant hand above the other. Put both thumbs on the club (not wrapped around) and slide your hands together.

Step 6

Ask students to describe the shape that is made with their legs as they set up to "address," or hit, the ball. The students might comment that the teachers' legs are shoulder-width apart and that her legs look like an upside-down *V*.

Ask students to notice how they are holding their arms as they have the club in the set-up position. Students might say that the golf club and their arms make the letter *Y*.

As this student prepares to practice his underhand swing, he will use learner SAY & DO to remember how to swing the golf club.

Step 7

After the students have practiced addressing (setting up) the ball, ask students to make up learner SAY & DO cues to remember how to position their bodies to address the ball before each swing. An example of cues might be APART (representing what the legs do) or DOWN (representing what the arms do).

Step 8

Have students practice setup and swing. Students need to be encouraged to use their learner SAY & DO words or cue words for setup before swing.

Step 9

Ask students to talk about what the club has to do during the swing. Students will share that the club must go back, come down, and go high. Ask each student to determine what words he or she wants to say for each of the three parts of a golf swing. For example, one student might use the words SWING, HIT, and THROUGH to describe his golf swing. Students practice swinging using their words as they do the movement (learner SAY & DO). This practice is being done without the ball.

Step 10

Send one student to each hitting station (one student to each golf tee). Assign each person at the hitting station a "retrieving" partner and send that student to the landing area. (If there are enough clubs for each student, then each student can hit and retrieve his or her own balls.)

Have the "hitting" partner take three practice swings on the tee mat. Then have this partner set the ball on the tee. Make sure he or she checks the area to see that it is safe to swing. Then have this partner swing to strike the ball. Repeat for a second ball. Have students put the club down when finished.

Step 11

Have partners switch places. The retrieving partner picks up the two balls on the way in to the hitting station. Repeat Steps 9 and 10.

Note: For Steps 9 and 10, if there are enough mats and tees for each person, have students do these steps without a retrieving partner. Everyone can do practice swings and hit balls. Students retrieve their own balls after everyone is finished hitting.

In this class, where there is enough equipment for each student in the class, students practice striking the golf balls.

Facilitation and Reflection

Ask students the following questions to help them reflect on their experiences and extend their thinking:

- *How do you grip the golf club?*
- *Describe what an underhand golf swing looks like.*
- *Why is visual tracking important?*

Extensions

- Set targets up at various distances to give students opportunities to explore swinging the club while working on the concepts of force, timing, and intensity to improve their accuracy.

29

Volleying (Bumping)

Students use a volleyball to explore the different ways they can volley the ball against the wall. Teacher and students use learner SAY & DO to work on the skill of bumping a volleyball.

Essential Question

What does volleying mean?

Curriculum Concepts

- Manipulative skill — volleying
- Timing
- Force
- Visual tracking

Physical Education National Standard(s)

Standard 1

Materials

- Volleyballs, one for each student
- Poly spots (flat, polyvinyl circles), one for each student
- Flat wall surface

Steps to Success

Step 1

Ask students the essential question "What does volleying mean?" Working in personal space alone, have students work on bumping and volleying the ball.

Step 2

Have students share how they bumped the ball, keeping the ball in personal space. Have students take turns as the leader while the other students in the class copy. After several students have been the leader, sharing the way they were bumping, ask the class "How were the volleys different or similar?"

Bumping and Volleying a Volleyball

Bumping — A method of propelling the volleyball in which the hands are connected and the forearms are together and extended forward to create a flat surface. Bumping involves striking the ball, using the area above the wrist to the middle of the forearm, while bending knees.

Volleying — Striking the ball up in the air continuously.

Bump pass — Using the skill of bumping to pass the ball in volleyball.

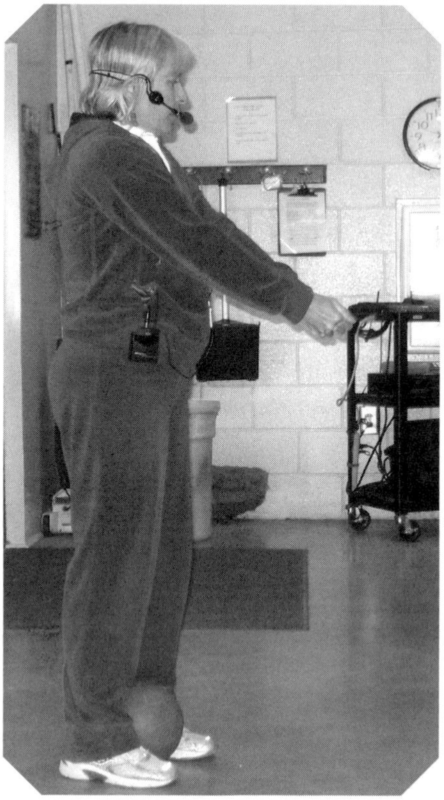

This teacher demonstrates how to make a fist with one hand and wrap the other hand around the fist, with arms and thumbs straight and flat, to get in position to bump the volleyball.

Using learner SAY & DO (TOSS-BUMP-BUMP-BUMP), these students practice continuous bumping of the volleyball.

Step 3

If a student has not shown the example of a bump (hitting the ball after putting palms of the hands together, making a fist with one hand and wrapping the other hand around the fist, with arms and thumbs straight and flat) then you may need to visually show students how to place their hands in position to bump the ball. Critical elements of the bump students should discuss include connecting hands, creating a flat surface with the hands, keeping arms straight and knees bent, using visual tracking (keeping your eye on the ball), and hitting square to the target.

Step 4

Ask students to watch as you toss the ball up (say TOSS), bump the ball (say BUMP), and then catch the ball (say CATCH). Repeat: TOSS-BUMP-CATCH. Have the students try this using learner SAY & DO.

Step 5

Show students continuous bumping using learner SAY & DO: TOSS-BUMP-BUMP-BUMP. Say BUMP every time the ball hits your forearms. Show students that if they lose control of the ball, they can stop and start over.

Step 6

As students get better at bumping the ball in personal space, they can try using a bump pass to the wall, with the ball coming back to them. (See the sidebar on p. 171 for a definition of a bump pass.)

Facilitation and Reflection

Ask students the following questions to help them reflect on their experiences and extend their thinking:

- *What did you learn about force, timing, and visual tracking?*
- *What are the critical elements of bumping a volleyball and performing a bump pass?*
- *How did using the learner SAY & DO strategy help you?*

Extensions

- Students get in pairs; one partner throws the ball underhand to the other partner. That partner uses a bump pass to get the ball back to her partner.
- The partners try to keep the ball off the floor by using the bump pass to pass the volleyball back and forth to each other.
- Put students in groups of three or four. Students use the skill of bumping to keep the ball up in the air continuously for as long as they can as a group. Students will want to keep count of the number of bumps they make before the ball lands on the floor or ground.

References

The American Heritage Dictionary, Second College Edition. (1985). Boston: Houghton Mifflin.

Epstein, A. S. (1993). *Training for quality: Improving early childhood programs through systematic inservice training.* Ypsilanti, MI: HighScope Press.

Jensen, E. (2000, November). Moving with the brain in mind. *Educational Leadership,* 34–37.

National Association for Sport & Physical Education (2003, Dec. 30). *Children need greater amounts of physical activity in 2004.* Retrieved June 10, 2009, from http://www.aahperd.org/naspe/template.cfm?template=pr_123103.html

National Association for Sport and Physical Education (2004). *National standards for physical education* (2nd ed.). Reston, VA: McGraw-Hill.

Piaget, J., & Inhelder, B. (1969). *The psychology of the child.* New York: Basic Books.

The Quotations Page. Quotations by Author. (n.d.) Albert Einstein. Retrieved August 28, 2009, from www.quotationspage.com/quotes/Albert_Einstein/

U.S. Department of Health and Human Services, Office of the Surgeon General. (n.d.) Surgeon General's call to action to prevent and decrease overweight and obesity. Retrieved August 28, 2009, from www.surgeongeneral.gov/topics/obesity/calltoaction

U.S. Department of Health and Human Services. (2008). *2008 physical activity guidelines for Americans summary, key guidelines for children and adolescents.* Retrieved October 28, 2008, from http://www.health.gov/paguidelines/guidelines/summary.aspx

Weikart, P. S. (2006). *Teaching movement & dance,* (6th ed.). Ypsilanti, MI: HighScope Press.

Musical Selections Provided With This Book

The following selections appear on the CD included with this book. Suggestions for appropriate activities are given for each selection.

Selections on CD	Suggested Activities (K–2)
Seven Jumps	1. Balance
Yankee Doodle	6. Fitness Routine
Joe Clark Mixer	11. Levels
Yankee Doodle	11. Levels
Peat Fire Flame	17. My Personal Space
Gaelic Waltz	23. Time: Fast or Slow?
Popcorn	23. Time: Fast or Slow?

Selections on CD	Suggested Activities (3–5)
Bele Kawe	4. Bele Kawe
Blackberry Quadrille	5. Building Sequences Using Locomotor Movement
California Strut	6. Close Encounters
Peat Fire Flame	11. Dribbling to a Steady Beat
Soldier's Joy	11. Dribbling to a Steady Beat
La Raspa	12. Dribbling With Feet
Fjäskern	14. Fjäskern
The Hustle	17. The Hustle
Rakes of Mallow	18. Irish Stew
Les Saluts	19. Les Saluts
O'Keefe Slide/Kerry Slide	21. Nonlocomotor Movement Sequences
Popcorn	22. Parachute Extravaganza

Glossary

activity extension — An activity that builds on a prior, related activity to extend children's skill development.

aerobic capacity — The capacity of the body's respiratory and cardiovascular systems to transport oxygen to working muscles.

alternating locomotor movement — A movement that requires transfer of weight from one foot immediately to the other foot (example, walking).

asymmetrical — When each side of the body is positioned differently.

balance — Stability produced by even distribution of weight on each side of the body's vertical axis.

basic timing/steady beat — The ability to independently feel, express, and keep the underlying steady beat of a rhyme, song, or musical selection with nonlocomotor and locomotor movement.

beat awareness — The ability to keep your own internal beat, to match someone's steady beat that is spoken or shown by using verbal or visual directions, and to perform nonlocomotor or locomotor movements to a rhyme, song, or recording selection.

beat competence — The ability to independently identify (feel), express, and keep the microbeat beat or macrobeat while using nonlocomotor or locomotor movement to a rhyme, song, or recording.

bump pass — Using the skill of bumping to pass the ball in volleyball.

bumping — A method of propelling a volleyball in which the hands are connected and the forearms are together and extended forward to create a flat surface. One strikes the ball, using the area above the wrist to the middle of the forearm, while bending the knees.

buoyant landing — The action of springing up quickly after a jump.

cardiovascular fitness — The capacity of the heart and lungs to supply oxygen-rich blood to the working muscles, and the capacity of the muscles to use oxygen to produce energy.

choreography — Taking movement patterns and sequencing them to music.

cognitive-motor links — A group of connected thought processes associated with a motor task.

complex alternating locomotor movement — A combination of two different weight transfers (example, skipping).

cooperation — The act of working together toward a common end, goal, or purpose.

creative movement — Starting with a movement and then changing it in some way.

defensive strategies — Movements or actions taken to protect or defend in sports.

do-si-do — A dance movement in which partners pass right shoulders then move back to place, passing left shoulders.

dynamic balance — A type of balance that involves maintaining an on-balance position while moving, starting, and stopping.

dynamic movement — A movement that continues without pausing.

***Education Through Movement (ETM)* teaching model** — Developed by Phyllis S. Weikart, the teaching model uses an approach of facilitating learning by working as a partner with children; the model includes the strategies of separate, simplify, and facilitate.

essential question — A key question used in the activities of this book to focus students' learning.

facilitate — A component of the *Education Through Movement* (ETM) teaching model in which the teacher uses varied strategies involving action, thought, and language to engage learners and enable them to construct their own knowledge.

fine-motor movement — Movement that requires a high degree of control and precision and generally involves small movements of the hands, wrist, fingers, feet, toes, lips, and tongue.
force — The capacity to do work or cause physical change; strength; power. In this book's activities, force refers to how hard an object is hit or struck.
general space — All the space within a room or boundary into which an individual can move by traveling away from the original starting location.
gross-motor movement — Movements that involve large muscle groups and are used when walking, running, sitting, crawling, etc.
hip bump — An action in which partners use their hips to make contact with one of their partner's hips.
hitting — The striking of an object.
hop — A movement characterized by a one-foot takeoff and same-foot landing.
integrated movement — Movement that involves moving two or more different areas of the body together purposefully at the same time.
inverted balance — A balance done upside down using any combination of equal weight on the hands, head, one foot, shoulders, or arm.
jump — A movement that involves taking off with two feet and landing on two feet, or jumping from one foot and landing on two; a jump is defined by the landing, not the takeoff.
layering — A teaching strategy in which teachers have students add a movement while the students are doing another movement they have already learned. For example, when teaching jumping jacks, teachers have students start by using only their legs, and after doing this sequence of leg movements several times, teachers have students "layer on" the arm movements without stopping the legs.
learner SAY & DO — A learning strategy that requires students to link each single movement they make to a single descriptive word (example: marching — each time one foot touches the ground, the student says the word MARCH).
learner THINK & DO — A learning strategy that is like learner SAY & DO and learner WHISPHER & DO, only students think the words instead of whispering or saying them.
learner WHISPER & DO — A learning strategy that is like learner SAY & DO and learner THINK & DO, only students whisper the words instead of using their voice.
LISTEN & DO — A learning strategy in which a person listens to a verbal direction and then performs the movement.
locomotor movement — Nonanchored movement consisting of transfers of weight in personal or general space (e.g., rolling, crawling, walking).
macrobeat — The accented first beat in a group of two or three beats.
microbeat — Each beat in a group of two or three beats; movements are done on each beat of the music.
moving with objects — Doing movements while holding objects; for example, running with a football, cutting paper, or playing a musical instrument.
muscle memory — The body's ability to automatically perform a well-rehearsed movement.
nonlocomotor movement — A movement done while a body part is anchored.
offensive strategies — Movements or actions done in sports to protect the ball and keep others from taking it away.
overhand set — In volleyball, an action in which the hands are above the head and palms are facing toward the ceiling; using the pads of the fingers, one makes contact with the ball and pushes the ball up in the air.
overhand throw — A throw performed with the opposite shoulder to the throwing hand facing the target; one steps into the throw with the foot opposite to the throwing hand.
pattern — A plan, diagram, or model to be followed.

personal space — The space around the body extending as far as the body and body parts can reach without touching other people or objects.

plan-do-review — A sequence in which students plan what they are going to do, carry out their plan, then recall what they did.

punt — A kick that is performed by releasing a ball from the hands and kicking it while it is in the air.

purposeful movement — A movement that a person thinks about and labels so that he or she moves in a planned and intentional way.

scissor — A forward kicking movement of the legs in which the kicks occur in sequence; one leg kicks forward while the weight is brought down on the other foot, under the body.

separate — A component of the *Education Through Movement (ETM)* teaching model in which the adult demonstrates *or* gives verbal directions *or* uses hands-on guidance.

sequences — Movements that follow one after another; three or more movements that continue in the same order.

sequenced movement — A movement set has two parts, with one movement followed by another; for example, *bend and straighten.*

set — In volleyball, when a player tries to place the ball near the net.

sideways swing — Swinging a racket, or bat, or paddle from the side of the body.

simplify — A teaching strategy that involves beginning with what is easy for students or manageable for them to process, allowing students to become immediately engaged and experience success.

single alternating locomotor movement — Movements often labeled with one word in which weight is transferred from one foot to the other; for example, running, marching, walking.

single movement — A movement that can be described using one word, for example, *step* or *hop.*

space awareness — An awareness of where and how the body moves.

static balance — A balance that involves maintaining a desired shape in a stationary position.

static movement — A movement that stops or pauses before a new movement is presented.

steady beat — The consistent, repetitive pulse that lies within every rhyme, song, or musical selection.

step — A transfer of weight from one foot to the other.

striking — Having the striking surface at the right place at the right time to make contact with an object.

symmetrical — Having both sides of the body positioned in exactly the same way.

synchronization — Two or more people organizing their movements to look identical.

timing — The coordination and regulation of movement needed to achieve the desired effect (for example, in some of the activities in this book, timing is required to make contact with an object).

underhand throw — A throw in which one faces toward the target and steps into the throw with the foot opposite to the throwing hand.

visual tracking — Following an object with one's eyes.

volleying — In some sports, when the ball stays in play for a long time.

walk — The easiest locomotor movement, which involves stepping forward with one foot and then with the other.

watch and copy — A learning strategy in which students watch the instructor demonstrate a movement and then imitate what the instructor did.

weight transfer — Shifting weight from one part of the body to another.

yielding landing — The action of bending one's knees to absorb the force when landing, as if sinking into the floor.

Subject Index

V

W

Appendix A: Reproducible Beat-Box Form

Appendix B: Complete Language-to-Dance Vocabulary

This chart includes all the language-to-dance vocabulary for the dances included in Chapter 5.

Language-to-Dance Vocabulary

Locomotor Movement (weight transfers)—one word equals one step
FORWARD, BACKWARD Moving one behind the other around the circle or in a line
IN, OUT Moving toward and away from the center of the circle
SIDE Moving sideward while facing center
BACK Crossing behind
CROSS Crossing in front
CLOSE Stepping next to the foot that has moved side, or in, or forward
TURN Turning the body on the step to face a different direction
STEP A transfer of weight in place
ACCENT A step with intensity

Nonlocomotor movement (non-weight-transfers)
TOUCH A movement of the foot against the floor
HEEL TOE A movement placing the heel/toe on the floor
KICK A movement of the leg in which the knee is straightened
LIFT A movement in which the knee remains bent
UP A movement in which the knee moves straight up in front of the body
STAMP A touch with intensity

(From *Teaching Movement & Dance,* by Phyllis S. Weikart, p. 79)

The Dance Language and Rhythm Pattern (Box Notation)*

In folk dance, the movement sequences correspond to the steady beats, creating a rhythmic structure for the dance. I have designed a notation system to represent a sequence of dance movements. To help students understand the time relationships of beat, divided beat, and rest, I use this small box

to represent the dancing beat, so a beat, a divided beat, and a rest can each be represented as follows:

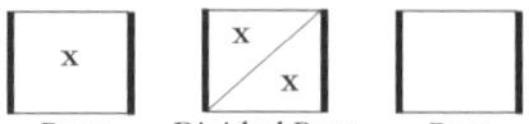

Beat   Divided Beat   Rest

With a series of 4 boxes, I can show 1 or more divided beats in a 4-beat sequence, such as in these examples:

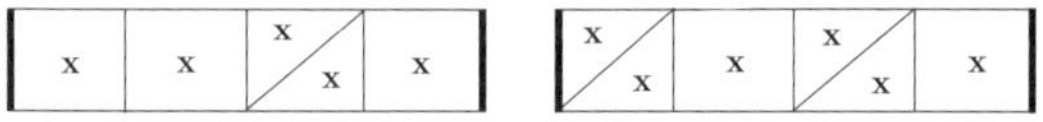

The rhythmic structure of each dance is represented by a series of boxes. Each box is equivalent to 1 steady beat of music—a macrobeat or a microbeat, depending on which of these the dance movements correspond to. For example, I use a series of boxes like this to represent 4 dancing beats of the music:

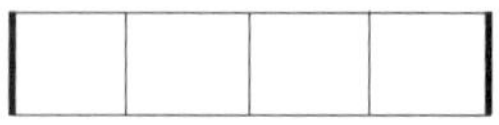

When a word occurs in a box, it indicates the locomotor or nonlocomotor movement for that beat. Four steps or movements to the underlying beat of the music can be shown like this:

IN	IN	IN	KICK

The divided beat, with two words in one box,

STEP/STEP

indicates that dancers are to do two steps or motions of equal duration (½ beat each), with the total of the two steps equaling a single beat. Thus, the following series represents one step toward the center (IN) on beat 1, another step toward the center (IN) on beat 2, two equal steps in place (STEP/STEP) that divide beat 3, and one step in place (STEP) on beat 4:

IN	IN	STEP/STEP	STEP

A box with no word in it signifies a rest (there is no movement for this beat). This series means dancers take one step each on beats 1, 2, and 3, and no step or movement (a rest) on beat 4:

IN	IN	IN	

A box divided into two unequal parts this way

indicates a beat divided into ⅔ and ⅓. When words occur in the box, as shown below,

FWD/HOP

dancers are to do one movement for the first ⅔ of the beat and then another movement for the last ⅓ of the beat.

The following abbreviations are used for the footwork notations:

- B A weight transfer to both feet
- (L) Nonlocomotor movement of left foot
- L Locomotor movement of left foot
- (R) Nonlocomotor movement of right foot
- R Locomotor movement of right foot

When one of the above letters occurs under a box, this designates the foot to be used for the step or movement on that beat.

The following series of boxes represents a 4-beat dance sequence requiring four locomotor movements using first the right, then the left, then the right, and then the left foot:

FWD	FWD	FWD	FWD
R	L	R	L

The following series of boxes represents a 4-beat dance sequence requiring five locomotor movements—moving the right foot on beat 1, moving the left foot on beat 2, moving the right and then the left foot on the divided beat 3, and moving the right foot on beat 4:

FWD	FWD	STEP/STEP	FWD
R	L	R L	L

The following series of boxes represents a 4-beat dance sequence—first one locomotor movement (IN) with the right foot on beat 1, next one nonlocomotor movement (KICK) with the left foot on beat 2, next one locomotor movement (OUT) with the left foot on beat 3, and finally one nonlocomotor movement (TOUCH) with the right foot on beat 4:

IN	KICK	OUT	TOUCH
R	(L)	L	(R)

In the box notation, the following abbreviations are used for words of the the Language-to-Dance Vocabulary:

FWD	FORWARD
BWD	BACKWARD
TOG	TOGETHER
CCW	counterclockwise
CW	clockwise
OPP. DIR.	opposite direction
OPP. FTWK.	opposite footwork
4X	four times
REPEAT	repeat the movements or steps in only the one row of boxes

*The material in this section is from *Teaching Movement & Dance,* by Phyllis S. Weikart, pp. 116–117.

Appendix C: Index of Related Activities

Movement Concept	K–2 Activities	3–5 Activities
Locomotor	6, 8, 12	5, 8, 15
Nonlocomotor	6	8, 21
Striking	2, 5, 21	9, 16, 26, 28
Balance	1, 24	2, 7
Position Words	3, 25	
Pathways	4, 18	
Folk Dance	6	4, 6, 14, 17, 18, 19
Force	7	
Jumping	9, 10, 13, 19	
Space Awareness	11, 16, 20, 23	1, 15, 25
Levels	11	25
Patterns/Sequences	14	
Body Awareness	15, 22, 23, 25	25
Following Directions	16	
Personal Space	17	
Basketball Shooting		3
Basketball Dribbling		10, 11
Soccer — Dribbling		12
Hockey — Dribbling		13
Throwing/Catching		15, 20, 27
Kicking		16
Timing		22
Punting		23
Volleyball — Overhand		24
Volleyball Bumping		29

Appendix D: Pumpkin Ball Pattern

Instructions:

1. Cut 6 pieces of fabric (using either the large or medium pattern), adding ¼" all around for seams.
2. Sew right sides together in ¼" seam.
3. Leave 1 seam open 4" in order to turn ball to right side.
4. Fill with poly-fiberfill.
5. Hand stitch seams closed.

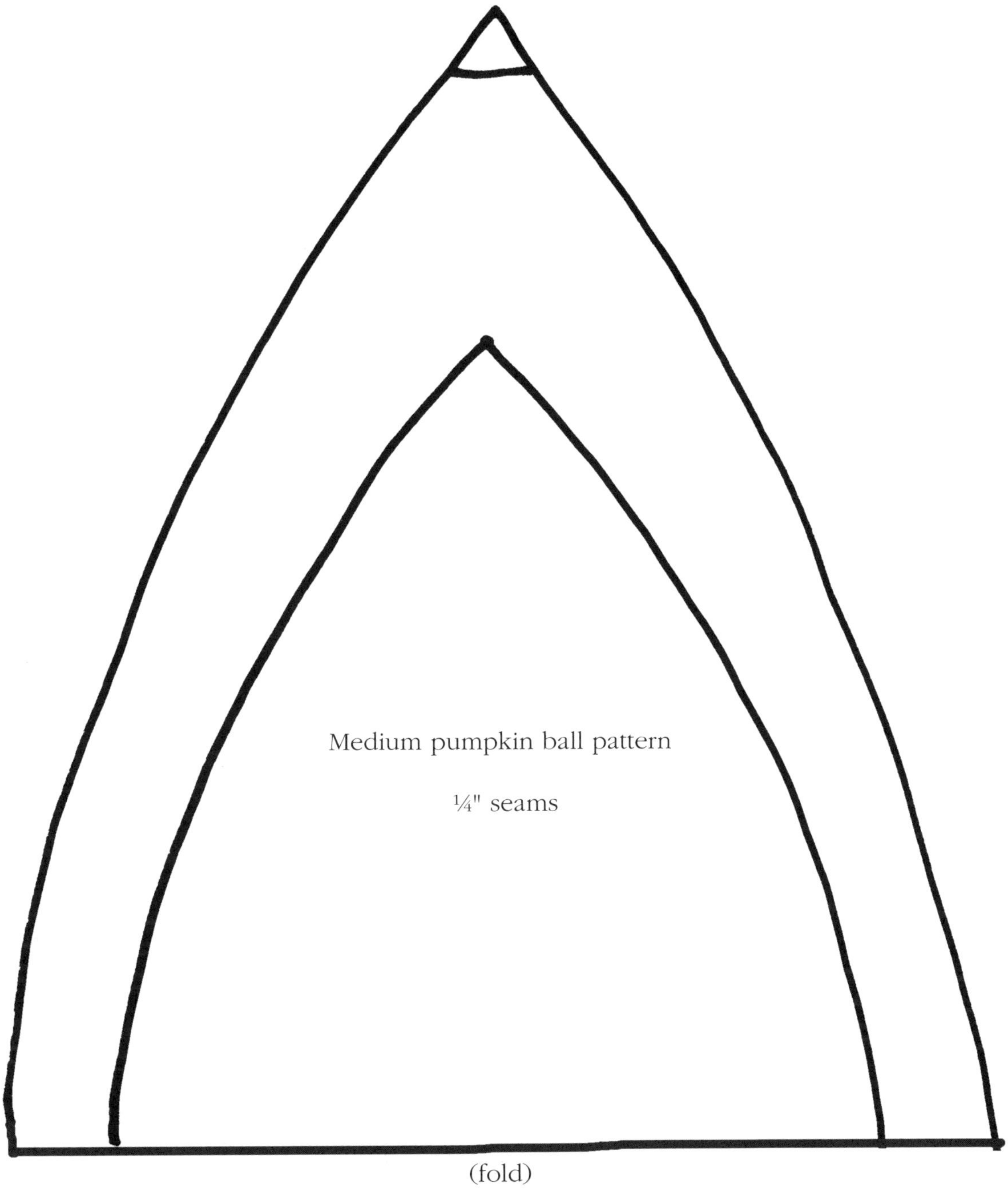

About the Authors

Karen S. Sawyers

Karen S. Sawyers is director of the Movement and Music Division of HighScope Educational Research Foundation. In this role, Sawyers directs training, curriculum development, and product development for HighScope's *Education Through Movement: Building the Foundation* program. Her training responsibilities include planning and conducting training events and coordinating HighScope's national network of movement and music trainers. Ms. Sawyers also serves as the project manager for the Ready School Assessment initiative. She is responsible for training, technical assistance, and product development associated with the Ready School Assessment tool.

Ms. Sawyers has presented at conferences throughout the United States serving early childhood, elementary, music, and physical education teachers, administrators, and district coordinators. She has been a contributing editor and author for *Activate! Music, Movement & More* magazine, published by Heritage Music Press.

Prior to her employment at HighScope, Ms. Sawyers attained the highest state teacher certification in Tennessee as a Career Ladder III teacher. Ms. Saywers worked in Springfield, Tennessee, for 17 years, teaching students from preschool through eighth grade. She taught physical education and also served as a coach, middle school athletic director, and principal intern during this time. She became associated with HighScope in 1996 as a trainer in the *Education Through Movement* network.

Sawyers holds a B.S. in physical education and health from Tennessee Tech University and an M.A. in Administration and Supervision from Austin Peay State University.

Linda Icaza

Linda Icaza has been a physical education teacher for 30 years. She has been working with *Education Through Movement* for 17 years and is an endorsed trainer with the program. She has taught students in the public schools in grades K–6 in Florida and Georgia. Ms. Icaza is past chair of the dance division of the Georgia Association of Health, Physical Education, Recreation, and Dance (GAHPERD). She is a graduate of Auburn University (B.S. in education, with a major in physical education, health, and recreation) and Piedmont College (M.A. in early childhood education). Ms. Icaza has presented at national and state physical education conferences. She has also presented workshops for educators in Georgia schools and for classes at Shorter College in Lawrenceville, Georgia.

Ellen Colley

Ellen Colley has been a physical education teacher in Pensacola, Florida, for 24 years. She has taught at the elementary level during her teaching career. She spent 13 years as softball coach at Pensacola Junior College. She received the Teacher of the Year award at Edgewater Elementary School in 1999. Ms. Colley was chosen Escambia County's Elementary Physical Education Teacher of the Year in 2003. She has worked with the *Education Through Movement* program since 2002. Ms. Colley is a national board certified teacher and is currently a field consultant for the Movement and Music Department of the HighScope Educational Research Foundation.

Resources From HighScope

Round the Circle: Key Experiences in Movement for Young Children, 2nd Ed.

Young children learn through play, and their play is full of movement experiences. *Round the Circle* has been completely revised to present the *HighScope Education Through Movement: Building the Foundation* program for preschoolers developed by Phyllis S. Weikart. This second edition presents *eight key experiences in movement* that help adults *engage, enable,* and *extend* children's active movement explorations. In addition, Weikart's teaching model provides a strong framework for encouraging and supporting young children's learning. Readers will appreciate the numerous *suggested activities, concrete guidelines,* and *effective teaching strategies* that are peppered throughout the book. Use this well-illustrated and easy-to-understand book to make the most of children's movement adventures!

BK-M1020

P. S. Weikart. Soft cover, 176 pages. 978-1-57379-096-3

Movement in Steady Beat — Learning on the Move, Ages 3 to 7, 2nd Ed.

The activities in this book will keep young children moving to the beat — and loving it! Infant-toddler caregivers as well as preschool and early elementary teachers will welcome the learning experiences that develop children's basic timing, language, vocabulary, concentration, decision making, and leadership abilities. The attached CD contains rhymes and action song recordings for many of the book's activities.

BK-M1023

P. S. Weikart. Soft cover, 108 pages, includes music CD. 978-1-57379-130-4

Movement Plus Music: Activities for Children Ages 3 to 7, 3rd Ed.

This revised and expanded book of activities and accompanying CD will enable you to provide many opportunities for children to experience the fun and creativity of music. While enjoying these activities, children will develop key abilities that are foundations both for physical and academic learning: steady beat competence, physical coordination, concentration, and the ability to process information and act on it. Eight basic activities are presented, with many variations for each. The activities may be used at group times, at transition times, or in outdoor group activities.

BK-M1027

P. S. Weikart. Soft cover, 36 pages, illustrated, includes music CD. 978-1-57379-214-1

Movement Plus Rhymes, Songs, & Singing Games, 2nd Ed.

A revised collection of engaging movement activities for children. These activities supplement those described in *Round the Circle* and provide age-appropriate movement experiences. Use them during large-group time, small-group time, or transitions. Includes CD with colorful, appropriate music to accompany activities.

BK-M1025

P. S. Weikart. Soft cover, 100 pages, includes music CD. 978-1-57379-066-6

Order online: *www.highscope.org*

Making Connections: Movement, Music, & Literacy — Learning on the Move, Preschool–Grade 2

Children naturally enjoy moving and making sounds, as anyone who has visited a playground knows. As teachers, we can use these innate abilities and build on them to create the foundational experiences children need to develop language and literacy skills.

Making Connections provides you with activities that help make these connections between children's natural abilities and the skills they need for success. The 60 activities in this book are planned around curriculum concepts in movement, music, and literacy and will keep your preschoolers or early elementary children moving and singing as they develop literacy skills.

Each activity includes an easy-to-follow plan, and activities are labeled so that teachers can quickly locate the activities best suited for the age level of their children. For preschool to grade 2. The attached CD contains recordings that complement many of the activities in this book.

BK-M1030

L. Haraksin-Probst, J. Hutson-Brandhagen, & P. S. Weikart. Soft cover, photos, 166 pages, includes music CD. 978-1-57379-319-3

85 Engaging Movement Activities — Learning on the Move, K–6

The activities in this book will keep your K–6 students jogging, hopping, swaying, rocking, marching, patting, making pathways, and moving in all kinds of ways as they learn. Classroom teachers, as well as specialty teachers in physical education, music, and recreation, will find this book to be a rich source of ideas for challenging and enjoyable movement experiences. The experiences are planned around key curriculum concepts in movement and music as well as in academic curriculum areas such as math and reading. And because these experiences develop students' basic timing, language abilities, vocabulary, concentration, planning skills, and capabilities for cooperative decision making and leadership, teachers will see learning effects that stretch across the curriculum. An easy-to-follow plan is given for each activity. The attached music CD contains recordings that may be used with many of the activities from this book.

BK-E3040

P. S. Weikart and E. B. Carlton. Soft cover, illustrated, 216 pages, includes music CD. 978-1-57379-125-0

75 Ensemble Warm-Ups: Activities for Bands, Choirs, and Orchestras — Learning on the Move, Grades 4–12

The newest addition to the Learning on the Move series, this book is a resource for conductors and directors of a variety of vocal and instrumental ensembles — from upper elementary choirs, Orff ensembles, and beginning bands to middle school and high school choirs, orchestras, and bands.

These active start-ups to ensemble rehearsals will result in more productive sessions as students explore, share, discuss, and discover the information necessary to be self-directed musicians. For grades 4–12. Free music CD included with book.

BK-M1024

P. S. Weikart, B. Boardman, & E. Bryant. Soft cover, 216 pages, CD included. 978-1-57379-144-1

Order online: *www.highscope.org*

Teaching Movement & Dance: A Sequential Approach to Rhythmic Movement, 6th Ed.

Written by Phyllis S. Weikart, one of the country's leading authorities on movement-based active learning and recreational folk dance, this revised and expanded edition offers improved teaching progressions to help students develop comfort with movement and steady beat independence. Featuring 134 step-by-step dance notations including more than 30 new dances, the sixth edition of *Teaching Movement & Dance* will prove valuable to music and physical education teachers, elementary classroom teachers, curriculum coordinators and supervisors, and persons working with older adults.

BK-M1029

P. S. Weikart. Soft cover, 489 pages. 978-1-57379-288-2

DVD Set

Beginning Folk Dances With Phyllis Weikart

This DVD collection of 134 folk dances taught by Phyllis S. Weikart, one of the country's leading authorities on international folk dance, was created so that people of all backgrounds and ages — from second graders to senior citizens — could learn and enjoy the wonderful experience of folk dancing. For each dance, there is a teaching strategies section taught by Phyllis, followed by a demonstration of the entire sequence performed by a mixed-age group of students. The dances are organized by motor development difficulty so they can be taught sequentially. The program includes a special section giving examples of the SAY & DO process that helps students improve their mastery of the dances, and demonstrations of basic folk dance steps and patterns, handholds, and formations. In this collection of 6 DVDs, Phyllis demonstrates her proven approach to teaching folk dance. Includes all the dances from Teaching Movement & Dance.

BK-M1031

6 DVDs, over 14 hours of footage, viewer guide included. 978-1-57379-347-6

Remastered Digital CDs

Rhythmically Moving 1–9

Music for students of all ages. Includes suggestions for use with *Teaching Movement & Dance: A Sequential Approach to Rhythmic Movement.* Can also be used with the *Beginning Folk Dances With Phyllis Weikart* DVDs and the *Teaching Folk Dance Successful Steps* video series and all other folk dance books from HighScope Press as well as the early childhood movement and music publications. Select one or all of these recordings. There is no special order or level of difficulty. Visit our Web site at highscope.org for complete song lists.

P. S. Weikart, creative director. CDs.

Rhythmically Moving 1 BK-M2401 1-57379-185-7
Rhythmically Moving 2 BK-M2402 1-57379-138-5
Rhythmically Moving 3 BK-M2403 1-57379-142-3
Rhythmically Moving 4 BK-M2404 1-57379-148-2
Rhythmically Moving 5 BK-M2405 1-57379-149-0
Rhythmically Moving 6 BK-M2406 1-57379-175-X
Rhythmically Moving 7 BK-M2407 1-57379-176-8
Rhythmically Moving 8 BK-M2408 1-57379-177-6
Rhythmically Moving 9 BK-M2409 1-57379-178-4

Order online: *www.highscope.org*